TWAYNE'S WORLD AUTHORS SERIES

A Survey of the World's Literature

Sylvia E. Bowman, Indiana University

GENERAL EDITOR

SPAIN

Gerald Wade, Vanderbilt University

EDITOR

Alfonso Sastre

(TWAS 155)

TWAYNE'S WORLD AUTHORS SERIES (TWAS)

The purpose of TWAS is to survey the major writers —novelists, dramatists, historians, poets, philosophers, and critics—of the nations of the world. Among the national literatures covered are those of Australia, Canada, China, Eastern Europe, France, Germany, Greece, India, Italy, Japan, Latin America, New Zealand, Poland, Russia, Scandinavia, Spain, and the African nations, as well as Hebrew, Yiddish, and Latin Classical literatures. This survey is complemented by Twayne's United States Authors Series and English Authors Series.

The intent of each volume in these series is to present a critical-analytical study of the works of the writer; to include biographical and historical material that may be necessary for understanding, appreciation, and critical appraisal of the writer and to present all material in clear, concise English—but not to vitiate the scholarly content of the work by doing so.

Alfonso Sastre

By FARRIS ANDERSON
University of Washington

Twayne Publishers, Inc. :: New York

Library of Congress Catalog Card Number: 78-125251

MANUFACTURED IN THE UNITED STATES OF AMERICA

Preface

Alfonso Sastre, born in 1926, is a major figure of Spain's post-Civil War theater. He is the author of twenty-three plays, numerous essays of dramatic theory and criticism, and various pieces of prose. Although he has found only limited commercial success in his native country, Sastre has attracted attention both in and outside Spain. He is one of a very small number of present-day Spanish writers who have been sensitive to artistic and intellectual currents of postwar Europe, and his work undoubtedly embodies the most imaginative innovations to be found in Spain's contemporary theater.

Because of his experimental dramatic forms, his departure from Spanish traditions, his intellectualism, and his revolutionary politics, Sastre has been treated with less than objectivity by Spanish critics, producers, censors, and theatergoers. The controversy that surrounds him frequently obscures the fact that he is a talented playwright, a perceptive critic, and a vigorous intellectual. In the present study I shall not concern myself primarily with Sastre's problems with Spanish censorship and commercialism—although these factors are by no means insignificant insofar as they have affected Sastre's career in the theater. My basic purpose is rather to illuminate the substance and evolution of Sastre's thought and dramatic art, through attention to what I perceive as the overall dialectical unity of his work. I should be quite pleased if this study were to serve the purpose of clarifying Sastre's invaluable importance to the postwar reconstruction of Spanish letters.

Unfortunately, most of Sastre's work has yet to be published in English. Therefore, unless otherwise indicated, translations from the original Spanish are my own.

FARRIS ANDERSON

Contents

Preface

Chronology

1. The Man, His Times, and His Philosophy 13

2. The Early Essays 20

3. The Later Essays 43

4. The Theater of Alfonso Sastre 64

5. The Dramas of Frustration 73

6. The Dramas of Social Realism 84

7. The Epic Phase 116

8. Sastre's Prose Works 133

9. Conclusion 144

Notes and References 147

Selected Bibliography 159

Index 163

Chronology

1926 February 20: Alfonso Sastre born in Madrid.

1930 Death of Spanish dictator Primo de Rivera.

1931 King Alfonso XIII abdicates; Spanish Republic declared.

1936 Spanish Civil War begins.

1939 End of Civil War; beginning of Franco regime.

1945 Sastre participates in the founding of an experimental theater group, Arte Nuevo (New Art).

1946 Sastre's first stage productions with Arte Nuevo: *Uranio 235* (*Uranium 235*) and *Ha sonado la muerte* (*Death Has Sounded*), the latter written in collaboration with Medardo Fraile. Sastre writes *Cargamento de sueños* (*Cargo of Dreams*).

1947 Sastre and Fraile write *Comedia sonámbula* (*Sleepwalker's Comedy*); it is not performed.

1948 *Cargo of Dreams* performed by Arte Nuevo. Sastre becomes theater editor of the new student magazine, *La hora*. Collapse of Arte Nuevo.

1949 Première of Antonio Buero Vallejo's *Historia de una escalera* (*Story of a Stairwell*): the first major work of Spain's postwar theater of social concern.

1950 Sastre and José María de Quinto issue a futile manifesto for a Theater of Social Agitation (T.A.S.). Sastre completes *Prólogo patético* (*Pathetic Prologue*).

1951 *Pathetic Prologue* rejected by the María Guerrero National Theater. Sastre completes *El cubo de la basura* (*The Garbage Pail*), and in December begins *Escuadra hacia la muerte* (*The Condemned Squad*).

1952 *Pathetic Prologue* again rejected by the María Guerrero. Sastre completes *The Condemned Squad* and begins *El pan de todos* (*Community Bread*).

1953 *The Condemned Squad* is produced by a university theater group at the María Guerrero Theater. The play is enthusiastically received. Even though it is ordered closed after three performances, Sastre's reputation as a major young dramatist has been established. Sastre finishes his university studies, completes *Community Bread*, and writes numerous pieces of dramatic criticism in various Spanish periodicals.

1954 *Pathetic Prologue* and *Community Bread* prohibited for stage production. Sastre writes *La mordaza* (*The Gag*), which is premièred in Madrid on September 17, under the direction of José María de Quinto. This is Sastre's first professional production; it has a successful run. Composition of *Tierra roja* (*The Red Earth*).

1955 Sastre writes *Ana Kleiber* (*Anna Kleiber*) and *La sangre de Dios* (*The Blood of God*); the latter is produced in Valencia. Writes *Muerte en el barrio* (*Death in the Neighborhood*) and *Guillermo Tell tiene los ojos tristes* (*Sad Are the Eyes of William Tell*); both are prohibited. Marries Eva Forest.

1956 Sastre writes *El cuervo* (*The Raven*). Birth of his first son, Juan. Publication of *Drama y sociedad* (*Drama and Society*). Imprisoned for political reasons.

1957 *Community Bread* premièred, with cuts, in Barcelona. Sastre himself orders the play closed after it is interpreted by many as an anti-revolutionary statement. Première of *The Raven* in Madrid. First issue of important Spanish theater magazine, *Primer acto.*

1958 Sastre writes *El Paralelo 38* (*The 38th Parallel*). Birth of his second son, Pablo.

1959 Serious interest in the theories of Bertolt Brecht. Composition of *Asalto nocturno* (*Nocturnal Assault*), *En la red* (*In the Net*), and *La cornada* (*Death Thrust*).

1960 Première of *Death Thrust* in Madrid and *Anna Kleiber* in Athens. Sastre and Quinto found the Realistic Theater Group (G.T.R.). Sastre is one of 227 Spanish intellectuals and artists who sign a public statement condemning censorship in Spain.

1961 The G.T.R. has its only successful season. Première by this group of *In the Net;* diplomatic repercussions lead to the play's prohibition for subsequent performances outside Madrid. Prémière of *Anna Kleiber* in Paris. Brief political imprisonment for Sastre.

1962 Birth of daughter, Eva. Sastre writes *Oficio de tinieblas* (*Office of Darkness*); it is prohibited. Begins work on *La sangre y la ceniza* (*The Blood and the Ashes*).

1963 Composition of *Anatomía del realismo* (*Anatomy of Realism*) and *Las noches lúgubres* (*Lugubrious Nights*). Publication of *Cuatro dramas de la Revolución* (*Four Dramas of Revolution*). Violent repression of striking miners in Asturias; Sastre and other playwrights are banned from Spain's national theaters because of their public protest of alleged atrocities against the miners.

1964 Publication of *Lugubrious Nights.* Journey to Cuba, to participate in a Festival of Latin-American Theater.

1965 Completion of *The Blood and the Ashes.* Unsuccessful attempt to obtain American visa in order to visit the U.S.A.
1966 Composition of *La taberna fantástica* (*The Fantastic Tavern*).
1967 Première in Madrid of *Office of Darkness,* under the direction of José María de Quinto; the play is received with little enthusiasm. Composition of *El banquete* (*The Banquet*).
1968 Composition of *Crónicas Romanas* (*Roman Chronicles*). Journey to Cuba.

CHAPTER 1

The Man, His Times and His Philosophy

I *Some Biographical Highlights*

THE Civil War that devastated Spain from 1936 to 1939 cut short an incipient renaissance of Spanish literature. From the present vantage point in history it seems clear that Spain, whose cultural life had been brilliant in the sixteenth and seventeenth centuries, and had then passed through two hundred years of relative eclipse, could again, in the early years of the twentieth century, boast a vigor in the arts unsurpassed by any other nation in Europe. This resurgence had first been embodied in the Generation of 1898, which included Miguel de Unamuno, and had been continued by the succeeding generation, of which Federico García Lorca was a notable representative. The political murder of Lorca in 1936 was to become a symbol of the fate of the arts in Spain during the coming years.

The Spanish society that emerged from the wreckage after 1939 has provided a difficult context for the artist, and in particular for the creative writer. Strict government censorship, a powerful Catholic Church, economic hardship, and national intellectual lethargy have combined to produce an atmosphere in which serious writers frequently leave the country, compromise their work, or abandon literature altogether. The dramatist especially, and consequently the Spanish theater, have suffered from these influences. Economics and censorship are more immediate facts of life in the theater than in other areas of the literary world, and the playwrights who have aspired to restore Spain's theater to its former dignity have found their paths encumbered by the frequently fatal obstacles of commercialization and governmental control.

Most dramatists have, in one form or another, abandoned the struggle. Alfonso Sastre is one of the few who have not. On the occasion of Ugo Betti's death in 1953, Sastre wrote admiringly of Betti's "productive and passionately involved life."[1] One could equally apply this description to Sastre's own life as it has related to Spain's artistic and intellectual life of the post-Civil War period. Author of twenty-three plays, one novel, one volume of short stories, one biographical essay, two books of dramatic theory, and hundreds of essays, Sastre has emerged as one of the few prolific and internationally significant figures of the postwar reconstruction of Spanish letters.

Alfonso Sastre was born in 1926, in Madrid. The unifying motif of his life has been a restless encounter with Spain's theatrical and political institutions, which in his mind are closely related. In 1945, before he had completed his university studies, Sastre participated in the founding of Arte Nuevo: "New Art," an experimental theater group which was to achieve a generally overlooked importance in the history of the Spanish theater. Composed mainly of university students, Arte Nuevo was founded for the purpose of offering an alternative to the stale, anachronistic trivia that dominated the Spanish stage during the 1940's, in the years immediately following the Spanish Civil War. In addition to Sastre, the charter members of the group were José Franco, Alfonso Paso, Medardo Fraile, José María de Quinto, José Gordón, Carlos José Costas, and José María Palacios. These young men sought reform and renovation in all aspects of the Spanish theater. They called for a fresh dramatic literature as well as for new methods of staging and acting. To these ends they wrote and produced their own experimental plays. Sastre contributed four short plays to the group's effort.

Arte Nuevo lasted approximately two years, before financial difficulties decreed its demise. One should not overestimate this group's immediate impact on Spain's professional theater, because apparently it had very little. Insofar as it failed to produce desired reforms in the Spanish theater, the movement was a failure. In an historical sense, however, Arte Nuevo is of major significance in the history of the Spanish theater. This idealistic experiment provided a training ground for young men who would later become important figures in the Spanish theater: Sastre, Paso, Quinto. Furthermore, the restlessness embodied in Arte Nuevo can be seen, historically, as the announcement of a major development that was soon to take place: the emergence in Spain of a serious theater of social concern, the most articulate exponent of which was to be Alfonso Sastre.

Late in 1948, shortly after the death of Arte Nuevo, Sastre

initiated a long, prolific career as an essayist. His first vehicle was a new student magazine entitled *La hora* (*The Hour*). Alfonso Sastre became this new publication's first theater editor. In subsequent years he was to publish hundreds of articles and essays in various Spanish periodicals: *Guía* (*Guide*), *Correo literario* (*Literary Mail*), *Cuadernos hispanoamericanos* (*Hispano-American Notebooks*), *Primer acto* (*Act One*), *Cuadernos para el diálogo* (*Notebooks for Dialogue*), and others. His favorite subject was to be the arts in all their respects, but especially the relations between art and socio-political questions.

In 1950 Sastre and José María de Quinto announced the founding of a new theater group, to be called Teatro de Agitación Social (Theater of Social Agitation) and represented by its initials: T.A.S. The project's manifesto, published in October, 1950, represented the climax of a long campaign for theater reforms previously waged by Sastre on the theater page of *La hora*.[2] With this project Sastre and his former companion of Arte Nuevo hoped to introduce to the Spanish public some major contemporary dramatists of Europe and America who were still unknown in Spain. As the group's name implies, particular plays and playwrights were to be selected for their presumed ability to stimulate the social awareness of the Spanish public—a function which the established professional theater clearly was not fulfilling. Some of the dramatists proprosed were Arthur Miller, Elmer Rice, Bertolt Brecht, Jean-Paul Sartre, Eugene O'Neill, and Armand Salacrou. Unlike Arte Nuevo, T.A.S. was not conceived as an amateur theater group, but rather as a serious attempt to incorporate socially sensitive drama into Spain's professional theater.

In their manifesto Sastre and Quinto made it clear that they were not proposing a "party theater"—a theater group to be used for the dissemination of a single political viewpoint—but rather a new theater which would encourage the audiences to think, in whatever terms, about basic social and political questions. Not surprisingly, this liberal explanation of "social agitation" was not sufficient to allay the apprehensions felt by Spanish censors when they found themselves confronted with a proposal to stage the work of leftist playwrights, with the avowed purpose of agitating Spain's social conscience. The T.A.S. project fell victim to official pressures before it ever went beyond the purely theoretical stage.[3]

The decade that followed the T.A.S. campaign was a turbulent period in Sastre's life. These years include his marriage to Eva Forest of Barcelona, and the birth of their first two children, Juan and Pablo. In 1953 *Escuadra hacia la muerte* (*The Condemned Squad*), one of Sastre's major works, was premiered in Madrid by a university theater group, then closed after three performances because of protests from military authorities. The following year Sastre enjoyed his first professional production: *La mordaza* (*The Gag*) was staged at Madrid's Reina Victoria Theater under the direction of José María de Quinto. The play was a success and Sastre's generation acclaimed him as their spokesman in the theater. In 1956 Sastre suffered his first arrest for political activities; he was imprisoned for a short time and later given "provisional liberty," without passport, for four years. In this same year he published his first book of critical essays, *Drama y sociedad* (*Drama and Society*).

Again in the company of José María de Quinto, Sastre attempts to launch yet another dissident theater movement. The year is 1960 and the group is the Grupo de Teatro Realista (Realistic Theater Group). Like its predecessors, Arte Nuevo and T.A.S., the G.T.R. had been conceived as a means of bringing vital, relevant theater to Madrid's audiences. Specifically, Sastre and Quinto wanted their group to be a vehicle for the promotion of Realism in its many forms. The formation of the G.T.R. can, in fact, be attributed to Sastre's intense interest during this period in the nature of Realism: an interest which is reflected in his essays and culminates in the publication of *Anatomía del realismo* (*Anatomy of Realism*) five years after the G.T.R. is founded. Thus, in addition to serving as a means of bringing serious theater to the Spanish stage, the G.T.R. was intended by its founders as "a theoretical and practical investigation of Realism and its forms."[4] The G.T.R. was somewhat more successful than its predecessor, T.A.S.: it not only published important documents on the Spanish theater but also brought to the professional stage, in 1961, three major works: *To Clothe the Naked* by Luigi Pirandello, *The Inkwell* by Carlos Muñiz, and *En la red* (*In the Net*) by Sastre.[5] However, the eternal obstacles of censorship and financial difficulties brought the group's activities to an end after one season.

Sastre had been a passionate admirer of Fidel Castro since the Cuban Revolution of 1959, and in the fall of 1964 he made his first trip to Cuba. The occasion was his participation in a Festival of Latin-American Theater. Since that time he has returned to Cuba, in 1968, to attend a Cultural Congress in Havana. Shortly after his first trip to Cuba Sastre was invited by Pennsylvania State University to give a one-semester seminar, but political complications prevented his receiving an American visa and he was consequently unable to accept this invitation to visit the United States. At the present time Sastre lives and works in Madrid's Barrio de la Concepción.

II *The Revolutionary Ideology*

Sastre forms part of a generation curiously situated in relation to the Spanish Civil War. Sastre and his contemporaries—Ignacio Aldecoa, Rafael Sánchez Ferlosio, Ana María Matute, Juan Goytisolo, Carlos Bousoño, Blas de Otero, José Hierro, José Monleón, Carlos Muñiz, Lauro Olmo, Alfonso Paso, José María de Quinto, and others—were children when Spain was devastated by civil war. Their adolescence evolved during the terrible early years of Spanish fascism and their adult life has transpired within the context of military dictatorship. In different ways these writers have responded to their history and circumstances, and their responses have constituted the various youthful directions of Spain's literature during the postwar period.

One of the most energetic reactions to war and oppression has surely been that of Alfonso Sastre, who has seen that man's individual dignity and social freedom are interdependent, and that liberty can be reconquered and maintained only through a varied and persistent assault upon the forces of oppression. Sastre's thought and work have been immediately inspired by his life in Franco's Spain, but in his probings he has transcended the peculiarities of his own personal situation. The central suggestion of Sastre's work is that human liberty is a prerequisite for human dignity, and that this freedom must be won and preserved through a relentless vigilance against the institutions that constantly grow up around man, threatening his liberty and capacity for self-assertion. Sastre's aspirations and accomplishments go beyond those of a mere revolutionary propagandist, because Sastre has been perceptive enough to see that freedom is a dialectical, rather than linear, reality. That is, he has realized that one cannot win one's social or political liberty once and forever, because even revolutionary movements become reactionary institutions if they are not constantly challenged and constantly renewed. Sastre thus envisions social freedom as a dynamic process which can exist only as a vital tension between order and anarchy.

At the philosophical level this tension becomes a balance between concern for man in existential terms on the one hand, and in historical terms on the other. One is called upon to evaluate and resolve the conflicts between individual conscience and political necessity, intellectual integrity and revolutionary dogma, personal emotions and collective spirit. Both in his values and in the polarity of his reference points, Sastre has thus confronted the world in an eminently dialectical manner. His intellectual evolution has featured a vacillation between nihilistic despair and constructive socialism. In his theories he has insisted that the drama provide a dual perspective of man and a balanced presentation of ideology. This dualism has been the context of Sastre's search for a synthesis whose aesthetic translation is Realism—a Realism that will recapture the complete personality of fragmented man. As a dramatist Sastre has sought to use this dialectical tension as a dramatic device and a source of agitation.

In short, Sastre has personally undergone, and has attempted to inspire in his audience, an emotional tug-of-war, a dialectical weighing of thesis and antithesis, a challenge to established values and institutions. The tradition from which he draws is not Spanish, but rather the twentieth-century literary Marxism of Lukács, Sartre, Brecht, and Weiss. These are the men who have most influenced Sastre's thought, and one of Sastre's undeniable contributions to contemporary Spanish intellectual life is the diffusion in Spain that he has given to these and other modern European thinkers. Sastre is clearly the most sophisticated figure of Spain's largely provincial postwar theater: a theater dominated by trite situation comedies, thunderous melodramas, and pseudo-philosophical platitudes. Sastre's failure to achieve commercial success in Spain is a direct result of his refusal to write these kinds of theater. It is extremely important to note, however, that this antagonistic attitude toward the Spanish theater is consistent with the ideology embodied in his plays and essays. That is, Sastre's revolutionary political attitudes are analogous to his resistance to established theatrical institutions. There is a tight unity between his philosophy and his life, in that he lives the revolutionary dialectic that lies at the heart of his written work.

The very nature of Sastre's dialectical probing of human reality dictates a diversity of themes and forms. Sastre's varied subject matter, and the ways in which he has treated it, will be the object of our consideration in the following pages. The great variety to be found in the work of this restless intellectual warns against making pat assertions about the nature of that work. However, one can and should see in Sastre's many themes and dramatic forms a unifying determination to clarify human reality, exalt human freedom, and promote intelligent theater. The fact that he has found no one posture adequate for this task is a tribute to his intellectual integrity and artistic versatility.

CHAPTER 2

The Early Essays

I *The Religious Crisis*

ALFONSO Sastre's first serious essays appeared in 1949, and his first book, *Drama y sociedad* (*Drama and Society*), was published in 1956. There is, thus, between the beginning of his career as an essayist and the publication of his first book, a period of some seven years during which Sastre wrote prolifically in various Spanish periodicals. Most of the important essays from this period were collected and republished in *Drama and Society*. Those not included in that book fall into the following general categories: (1) Essays whose central ideas are also expressed in *Drama and Society*; (2) Articles which comprise a national and international chronicle of theatrical personages and events; (3) Repeated criticism of the theater in Spain and frequent recommendations for its improvement; (4) Reviews of books and films.

An aspect of Sastre's early thought which, unfortunately, is not reflected in his first book is the religious crisis so apparent in Sastre's writings through the year 1953. These early essays reveal an embryonic form of what would become the prime constant of Sastre's thought: an insistence on fluidity and agitation, a restless sensitivity to the relative nature of human values. In Sastre's later years this mentality would take the form of the ever-present *dialéctica* of his writings. In the early 1950's it is visible as a struggle with the absolute values of a Catholicism which Sastre would later abandon, but whose effects would continue to be present in his mature writings. There is an obvious contradiction between the advocacy of a moral absolutism on the one hand and the preachment of life's relativity on the other. Sastre has never rid his thought of this inconsistency. One might say that Sastre's entire intellectual evolution has been a search for something to fill the vacuum left by the disintegration of his Catholicism, which proved untenable in the world as Sastre perceived it. José María de Quinto explains Sastre's dialectic in this way: "Sastre transcended Catholicism to Christianity, and from Christianity he has gone to atheism. There was a moment when Sastre was on the verge of nihilism, but he has always controlled this tendency—at least, in his dramas."[1]

As we shall see below, it is doubtful that Sastre has "always" controlled his nihilistic tendencies. However, Quinto's statement does give an essentially accurate picture of Sastre's trajectory. In his attempt to find a point of equilibrium somewhere between anarchy and dogmatism while keeping both these extremes clearly in view, Sastre has become a political radical. The contradiction in Sastre's early values is an antecedent to his Marxism, which preaches the need for change while insisting on a rigid moral puritanism. It is also the point of departure for the socialist-existentialist duality and the aesthetic of agitation which Sastre develops, in theory and practice, through the coming years.

Through the year 1953, Sastre's dialogue is primarily with himself, and its starting point is his Catholic background. It takes the form of a verbal affirmation of his own continuing Christianity, a tendency toward puritanical dogmatism, and an attempt to reconcile both with his growing belief in the need for intellectual flexibility. It might be said that during the early 1950's Sastre was a victim of the very agitation which he would later attempt to impose on others.[2] In one of his many early attacks on Madrid's theater, Sastre scornfully bemoans the fact that the city's experimental groups are composed of "snobs" and "effeminate men" who are motivated by a "silly curiosity (usually perverted and unhealthy)." These people are, according to Sastre, "useless" for the theater.[3]

Sastre's irrational puritanism, and more directly his contention with Christianity, are analogous to a fundamental point of dramatic theory which unfolds for Sastre during those early years: the dramatist's responsibility and obligation to "engage" himself in the issues of his time. Sastre feels an inclination to cling to the puritanism and Catholicism of his formative years. In theory, however, he rejects the suggestion that the dramatist should align himself in a propagandist way with any predetermined set of moral values. Sastre's confusion and contradictions are made even greater by his exposure during these years to Jean-Paul Sartre's doctrine of *engagement* for the writer. Thus, in examining several of Sastre's essays written between 1951 and 1953, one notes the contradictions which result from their author's confusion. In opposing a proposed Festival of Catholic Theater in 1951, Sastre makes a rather unconvincing attempt to reconcile the dogmatism of the *engagement* with the theater's freedom from propagandist uses: ". . . I am not one of those who call for 'aesthetic purity' in the theater. I believe the dramatist should adhere to some ideology, even at the expense of the objectivity of his testimony and the 'artistic' purity of his work. But there should be no *a priori* criterion that pushes us in one direction or the other."[4] A "Catholic theater," Sastre maintains, can be only a "theater of Catholic propaganda and agitation. . . ."[5] This he objects to, contradicting his simultaneous assertion that the responsible writer must attach himself to an ideological point of departure.

In 1952 Sastre reiterated his reservations concerning the writer's *engagement*. He had by this time fallen quite under the influence of Jean-Paul Sartre, but he was disturbed by some of the overtones which the concept of *engagement* held for him. He thus felt compelled to reject explicitly the danger of arbitrary dogmatism which lay inherent in the doctrine of *engagement*: "The danger of political '*engagement*' is blindness to the possibility that the adversary may be right. . . . The '*engagement*' must be based on an objective vision of socio-political realities. It should not be based on a preconception; otherwise, reality will inevitably be distorted."[6] An "objective political *engagement*" is clearly a contradictory concept—one of the many to be found in Sastre's early essays. Sastre's vacillation over political *engagement* and his mistrust of "Catholic" theater are two aspects of the same dilemma.

Late in the year 1953 Sastre published two articles which reveal clearly their author's growing struggle with the Christianity of his youth. Sastre writes of Christianity in terms of its dramatic possibilities and concludes that they are many: "The conflict between society (the world) and Christian truth is . . . a situation that could be the subject of a tragedy . . ."[7] Man's futile longing for Truth—i.e., for Christ—carries an inherent dramatic conflict which, Sastre feels, could be effectively represented on the stage. Indeed, Sastre maintains that he himself attempts to write such a drama: "All that—the tragedy of a world without Christ, the tragedy of a world with its back turned to truth—is what I would call 'Christian drama.' That is the drama that I, in my humble way, try to write."[8] Sastre rejects, however, the suggestion that such a drama has already been realized and insists that the world is still awaiting the advent of "Christian drama" which will depict the tragic gulf between the world and Christian truth.

It is interesting that Sastre pays lip service to his own continuing Christianity while denying that the Christan vision of man has ever made a meaningful impact on the theater. He is reluctant to abandon Christianity, in spite of his growing pessimism as to Christianity's feasibility in modern society. He sees the Christian as an intruder in a society which is nominally Christian but whose values are actually far removed from those of Christianity: "The Christian is an outsider in a corrupt society that distorts and exploits the Christian doctrine. The Christian is frequently a scandalous figure in a 'Christian' society."[9] In short, Sastre attempts to cling to Christianity while denying its effectiveness.

After 1953 Christianity's viability ceases to be a major concern in Sastre's writings, but the tensions implicit in his early ideological struggles continue. Throughout the coming years, as the man's thinking grows more sophisticated, his youthful confusions and self-contradictions evolve into a deliberate cultivation of "dialectical" theater. With his aesthetic of agitation, a more mature Alfonso Sastre would later urge his audience to face the contradictions of its beliefs, just as he, as a restless young man, had been unable to overlook the contradictions of his own.

II Drama y sociedad (Drama and Society)

In the prologue to *Drama and Society* Sastre makes his intentions quite clear: His motives for writing this book were a desire to find an ultimate justification for all theatrical activity, and an awareness of the need for such a book in Spain. The Spanish drama critics, who logically should have attempted to establish a theoretical framework for their own activities, had shown no inclination to do so; thus, Sastre took upon himself the task of combating the lack of dramatic theory in Spain.[10]

Drama and Society is not a completely original piece of work. Three of its four parts consist of previously published articles, and the one section written especially for inclusion in the book is an extension and development of ideas for which Sastre had long been known in Spain. Sastre did not exaggerate the importance of his book when he stated that it was virtually unique in contemporary Spanish letters. *Drama and Society* has a definite importance in the history of Spain's postwar theater. In a consideration of Sastre's dramatic theories, the book is significant as a cogent summary of the author's thought from 1949 to 1956.[11]

In addition to explaining the motivation that led him to write the book, Sastre includes in his prologue a clear statement of intent. Possibly as a defense against anticipated criticism, Sastre asserts that his book is not intended to be a scholarly, systematic presentation of dramatic theory or information, and he expresses his hope that *Drama and Society* will serve as a basis or inspiration for a more systematic work which is still needed in Spain.[12] The book is, in fact, precisely what its author says it is: an unsystematic collection of largely impressionistic essays which are unified only by their author's passionate dedication to a health-restoring examination of the theater in general, and of Spain's in particular. One reviewer gave a summary of the book's strengths and weaknesses: "*Drama and Society* is a book bubbling with ideas: ideas spelled out with insight and conviction. But Alfonso Sastre should have employed a more rigid structure, a more coherent plan. This would have helped the book greatly. However, this is more a question of the book's form than its content. We repeat that it is a fiine book that deserves much discussion and thoughtful consideration."[13] This critic either did not realize or chose to ignore the fact that *Drama and Society* consisted largely of selected, previously published material, and he was obviously not impressed by Sastre's defense of the book's loose structure. In spite of its capricious organization, however, *Drama and Society* is of prime importance as a summary of Sastre's early thought and an anticipation of his future ideas about the drama.

The four parts of *Drama and Society* are entitled, respectively: "The Drama," "The Drama and Society," "The Drama in Spain," and "The Dramatists Die." The first part is original; the other three consist of previously published articles. Part III deals with problems peculiar to the theater in Spain; it is interesting as an indication of Sastre's rebellious attitude toward the mediocrity of Spanish theater, but it does not properly belong to the realm of dramatic theory. Part IV is a series of tributes to five recently deceased playwrights, all of them non-Spanish except for Enrique Jardiel Poncela. These pieces are essentially impressionistic musings on each dramatist's career and contribution to the theater. The playwrights saluted—Maurice Maeterlinck, Henri Lenormand, Enrique Jardiel Poncela, Ugo Betti, and Eugene O'Neill—had previously been the objects of Sastre's attention in other essays.[14] Sastre's perspective of the deceased dramatists is somewhat indicative of his own personal values. He sees O'Neill as a modern giant who, in spite of the "critical scandal" caused by some of his plays, fought to "restore the greatness of tragedy in our time."[15] Sastre is quite impressed by O'Neill's fundamentally tragic concept of human existence, and he regards the bulk of O'Neill's work as "the anguished testimony of his perpetual metaphysical crisis."[16]

Henri Lenormand, whom Sastre has repeatedly recognized as one of his major youthful sources of inspiration, is presented in much the same light as O'Neill. Lenormand was, according to Sastre, a testimonial dramatist who opted for "the real world (the world of his time)" in preference to "the world of imagination or poetic evasion" (*DS*, 191). As such, he should be regarded as a precursor of the Theater of Anguish which Sastre saw as the most significant direction of the theater in the 1950's. Lenormand was not generally thus considered by historians of the French theater and was, therefore, the "victim of clumsy, unjust critics. Not that the critics made erroneous judgments: they simply failed to make . . . obvious statements that they should have made. There is a sin of omission" (*DS*, 190). The oblivion into which Lenormand fell during the last years of his life constituted for Sastre "an unforgivable literary injustice."[17]

Enrique Jardiel Poncela, who died in 1952, was a Spanish writer of avant-garde comedies. His theater has little in common with Sastre's. Nevertheless, Jardiel is the object of Sastre's profound affection and respect. As in the cases of O'Neill and Lenormand, Sastre sees Jardiel as a superior and courageous figure whose life and career were defined by the adversities which this author was forced to suffer at the hands of mediocre contemporaries.

It is apparent that one of the reasons for Sastre's interest in these playwrights is his belief that all of them were, in some way, dissidents. Even though their dialectic with the status quo was partially negative and involuntary, they nevertheless represented a countercurrent. They were, each in his own way, rebels in their society and in the particular circumstances of their dramaturgy. Jardiel Poncela's opposition to prevailing trends in Spanish theater—and, by extension, in Spanish society—is implied for Sastre in that writer's failure to receive his due recognition. Likewise, Lenormand was the victim of unjust critics who had failed to grant him his rightful place in the history of the French theater. O'Neill, in addition to having provoked "critical scandal," is regarded by Sastre as the point of departure for all modern tragedy. The central point of *Drama and Society* is that tragedy is, by definition, a dissident, disturbing genre which, in modern times, implies social protest and the need for change. And, as noted above, Sastre was impressed by Betti's dedication, or *engagement*, which likewise implies agitation of consciences.

Thus, except for his piece on Maeterlinck—a slightly lyrical, noncommittal tribute to an author whose work Sastre did not admire—Sastre's pages on selected deceased dramatists emphasize the tensions of those careers. These brief essays and their antecedents are undoubtedly simplistic, but there is a significance in the perspective with which Sastre views each dramatist. The attention Sastre gives to tension and agitation in the careers of other writers is consistent with the primary place of this same theme in his own life, his theater, and his more purely theoretical essays.

Some of those theoretical essays constitute the first two parts of *Drama and Society*. An essential aspect of these writings is the above-mentioned contradiction, so fundamental to Sastre's thought. Although its terms have been modified somewhat, the contradiction of *Drama and Society* is the same one noticed in Sastre's earlier years. Sastre demands responsibility and commitment of the playwright, but he simultaneously rejects the theater's use for propagandist purposes. In effect, he opposes the preachment of absolute values from the stage. Apparently, Sastre vaguely senses that in order to be involved in social struggles, one need not necessarily embrace an ideology. It is difficult to accept this suggestion, for to be "committed" is to be committed to *something*. In Sastre's mind it is to be involved in the struggle for social change, but he hesitates to abandon the theater to this mission for fear that the result will be unilateral propaganda in support of a predetermined ideology.

Sastre's implicit self-contradiction is especially obvious in Chapters 8 and 9, Part II, of *Drama and Society*. In dealing with the relation between theater and social revolution, he vaguely suggests that the theater has been a companion to much social turmoil of modern times: the Russian and Mexican Revolutions, and American social unrest of the twentieth century: "The theater is a good companion for the revolution . . . on the stage, social anguish resounds and revolutionary groups, through the words of the playwright, express their hope in the new order. These are the two faces of political theater: on the one hand, revelation of horror and misery; on the other, hope in new social structures" (*DS*, 113). Sastre sees *engagement*, or involvement, as a condition for respectable dramaturgy, but he simultaneously places conditions on the dramatist's commitment to a political cause; conditions which would actually prevent the cultivation of revolutionary theater. "The *engagement* must be based on an objective vision of socio-political realities, rather than on a preconception, destined to distort these realities. An *engagement* based on preconception is unacceptable, not only for the theater, but for any social activity, artistic or otherwise" (*DS*, 114).

Here Sastre has fallen into self-contradiction. Revolutions are not designed and carried out by men who are "objective" in their view of society, but rather by persons passionately dedicated to a chosen ideology. Societies are not torn down and reconstructed because they violate some mythical code of absolute standards, but because some elements within the society would prefer that it were different. Sastre's notion of an "objective" *engagement* is itself a contradiction in terms. There is nothing objective about the "hope in the new order" which characterizes a revolutionary movement. Moreover, the "revelation of horror and misery," which the revolutionary playwright would presumably produce, would be possible only if the playwright, with a personal vision that negates objectivity, had previously decided that horror and misery did exist.

The same contradiction appears also in Chapters 1 and 3 of *Drama and Society*'s second part. The "committed" writer—i.e., the writer who cultivates "Social Realism"—is presented as one who gives primary value to the social resonance of his work and who realizes the secondary place of "artistic" values. But, according to Sastre, he does so while maintaining his reluctance to become personally dedicated to a particular cause: "Usually without going so far as to subscribe to particular political or religious doctrines, he attempts to stimulate prepolitical states of emotion and awareness—states which frequently encourage a purifying political action" (*DS,* 71). In paraphrasing Upton Sinclair and expressing his adhesion to that writer's attitudes toward literature, Sastre concurs that literature's function is to change the world, that "the real purpose of art is to modify reality" (*DS,* 78-79). Furthermore, in his advocacy of "committed art," Sastre accepts Sinclair's affirmation that "all art is propaganda . . . sometimes unconsciously, but usually deliberately" (*DS,* 80). These assertions suggest an adherence to an art totally dedicated to the advancement of a preconceived social ideology. Sastre's reluctance to approve of an absolutist *engagement,* revealed in other chapters of *Drama and Society* and elsewhere, is not apparent as he paraphrases and concurs with Upton Sinclair.

Essentially, Sastre's contradiction as reflected in *Drama and Society* consists of a hope for profound change without absolute conviction, hope for revolution without dogmatism. There are several possible explanations for this inconsistency. One is the very nature of *Drama and Society.* Because it is largely a collection of diverse essays, written at different moments and under varying circumstances, the book suffers from the lack of cohesiveness which characterized the composition of much of its material. If *Drama and Society* had been the result of a single sustained effort, much of its ideological contradiction might well have been resolved in the process of its composition. This speculation is supported by the observation that the inconsistency is far less prominent in the book's first part, which does consist of original material. Also, it appears that Sastre was excessively impressed by his readings during the early 1950's, and that the inconsistencies of *Drama and Society* are at least partially due to its author's failure to digest these multiple influences and to resolve the differences among them. Paradoxically, one of the strengths of *Drama and Society* is its echo of such diverse figures as Aristotle, Unamuno, Upton Sinclair, Arthur Miller, Eugene O'Neill, and Jean-Paul Sartre. It does appear, however, that this book's impressionable young author was overly anxious to make use of all his readings, and that in so doing he failed at times to subject them to a unifying distillation.

It must be stressed that although Sastre does not succeed in eliminating one of the terms of his ideological contradiction in *Drama and Society*, the inconsistency is a minor aspect of the book. It is admittedly annoying, and it reduces the book's significance as cogent dramatic theory, but the fundamental tendency of *Drama and Society* emerges clearly and strongly in spite of the work's inherent contradiction. The two terms of Sastre's contradiction as reflected in *Drama and Society* are commitment to a preconceived ideology and an aesthetic of agitation. The latter emerges obviously as the stronger element. Sastre's insistence on the constant dialectic is so predominant in *Drama and Society,* that his occasional concessions to an absolutely committed art appear, taking *Drama and Society* as a whole, as a hesitant homage to outside influences which Sastre respected but did not entirely accept. Sastre did not recognize the contradiction of *Drama and Society* and therefore made no visible effort to resolve it. Nevertheless, it is possible that the resolution lies implicit in the book itself, and more obviously in Sastre's thought on a larger scale. Despite his token approval of propagandist art, the commitment which Sastre favors in *Drama and Society* and elsewhere seems really to be a responsible dedication to an art which will challenge its public's values and stimulate its conscience. In this sense the commitment would be only to integrity, analysis, and agitation. The propagandist aspect of such an attitude would be relative to the circumstances of the moment and would preclude absolute loyalty to a particular political stance. This is Sastre's fundamental implication in *Drama and Society,* in his other theoretical writings, and in his theater.

Sastre's basic postulate, then, is that the theater should agitate and disturb. Indeed, the very title of *Drama and Society* is a reference to the theater's capacity for social agitation. With varying degrees of subtlety Sastre approaches this notion from several directions via a series of attitudes, some of which are synonymous and all of which are related: a scorn for aestheticism, opposition to propaganda, and advocacy of dynamic art, which includes "penetrative realism," theater of anguish, testimonial theater, existential theater, and tragedy.

Sastre's rejection of aestheticism is the converse of his conviction that the function of art is moral rather than decorative. In this regard his attitude coincides with his general aesthetic of agitation. Here, however, as in many instances, it must be noted that while the particular attitude is valid in terms of Sastre's basic premises, Sastre has delineated and defended his attitude in a naïve, simplistic way. He resoundingly rejects "beauty" as the purpose of art, but he does not define this term for his readers. In his mind there seems to be a general identification of several concepts which actually are not at all synonymous: "art for art's sake," surrealism, dehumanization, and "beauty." Furthermore, his presentation of this argument is based essentially on a simplistic cliché: a distinction between the aesthetic of Oscar Wilde ("art for art's sake") and that of Cesare Zavattini, whose reasons for writing were "moral" rather than "aesthetic" (*DS*, 73-75).

We have discussed above Sastre's theoretical opposition to propagandist theater as it relates to his concomitant and contradictory implication that the theater should project absolute values which may indeed constitute propaganda. In an early article, not included in *Drama and Society,* Sastre had written: "According to respectable Aristotelian principles, the plot is the beginning and, as it were, the soul of the tragedy. This is still true. In good theater the plot comes before the ideas. The ideas spring forth from the plot, and the characters define themselves through the plot."[18] He admits a valid distinction to be made between thesis plays based on "ideas" worthy of consideration and those which are intellectually poor, but this consideration pertains only to the intellectual substance of the play. Dramatically, no good play can be constructed on a preconceived ideological basis.

Here, as well as in *Drama and Society,* Sastre's objection to propagandist theater is its violation of the Aristotelian primacy of plot. In *Drama and Society* he reiterates his fear of the dramatist's "ideas": "Writing plays is . . . something radically different from expressing one's own ideas. . . . From a dramatic point of view, it is preferable that the author not have a rigid ideology and that he not be dogmatic. The author's dogmatism may undermine . . . the drama's objective purity" (*DS*, 123-24). Although Sastre announces categorically that in modern times "social matters" have emerged as the "supreme category of human concern,"[19] he insists that concerns for man's social welfare do not necessarily lead to propagandist theater: ". . . *social themes* are not necessarily proletarian themes" (*DS*, 128).

In the foregoing notions it is possible to see another suggestion of contradiction in Sastre's thinking. One may wonder whether it is really possible to reveal and comment on social injustices in a nonpropagandist way, and whether the very selection of phenomena to be revealed does not imply a predisposition which negates objectivity. Regardless of this possible flaw in his reasoning, it becomes increasingly clear that Sastre's ideal is an objectivity—a detachment—that will permit the playwright greater effectiveness in stimulating the awareness of his audience. By avoiding partiality in his presentation of the dramatic conflict's two sides, the dramatist will call attention to the struggle between the drama's opposing forces; if he favors one force over the other, the drama degenerates into propaganda, and the struggle —the very source of spectator agitation—is obscured by the prominence of the favored ideology. There is an implicit paradox in the assertion that detachment enhances penetration: a paradox that finds its expression in Sastre's ideological vacillation between commitment and independence for the dramatist. Thus, what initially appears as an annoying rational inconsistency becomes an interesting paradox of aesthetic theory.

Sastre's principle of "detached penetration" is expressed in four concepts which are, in essence, identical: theater of anguish, penetrative realism, testimonial theater, and existential theater. The theater of anguish is theater which reflects the anguish of human existence via a basically realistic technique: "It is the truly tragic current of the modern theater, constructed on the principles of Realism. It is the theater that extracts the awesome timelessness of existence, without evasive fantasy or magic. . . . This is the current cultivated by the great 'testimonial dramatists': those writers whose work is a testimony of reality" (*DS*, 154-55). The term "penetrative realism" refers primarily to the dramatic technique which will presumably be employed in the composition of theater of anguish. Again, emphasis is placed on "testimony," or documentation: "The artistic mode is indicated by the term 'Realism.' The writer or the artist becomes a witness . . . of reality. He selects, penetrates, and elaborates, in accordance with the creative impulse. Realism makes certain demands: it prohibits 'escapism' and the literature of 'poetic' or transformed reality" (*DS*, 71-72).

It is significant that Sastre regards the French director André Antoine as the fountainhead of modern Realism—the theater's fundamental direction in the twentieth century, according to Sastre (*DS*, 101-3). Antoine's Théâtre Libre is credited with having brought forth the "message of Realism": a passion for documenting human existence which has evolved into the "penetrative realism" of the contemporary testimonial theater.

> André Antoine, the pontiff of Naturalism in the theater, brings a purely descriptive, positivistic Realism. The *Théâtre Libre* works to bring reality faithfully to the stage. It aspires to work outside conventions and theatricalism. . . . The *Théâtre Libre* insists on the description of reality just as it appears in life. It brings to the theater a new discipline capable of leading us to reality itself, without contrived distractions. The *Théâtre Libre* unknowingly discovers the most authentic, and only valid, direction for the theater in the twentieth century. (*DS*, 102-3)

One may fairly ask what is to be the subject matter of this testimonial documentation so strongly advocated by Sastre. What is that which is to be documented via a realism which, hopefully, becomes "penetrative"? It is undeniable that Sastre's obvious concern is for man's relations with his fellow human beings, and his selection of the term "Social Realism" calls attention to this aspect of his thought. With characteristic caution, however, Sastre refuses to equate a social intent with a propagandist aim. The dramatist's intent should not be to propagandize in favor of a particular solution to social injustices, but rather to disturb his spectator by making him aware of the conditions of his existence. Such a revelation will presumably shake the spectator's consciousness to the extent that he will be disposed to undertake reparatory political action of his own choosing. The function of the drama, then, is "prepolitical" rather than political: ". . . it tries to stimulate a prepolitical condition in the audience's emotions and perceptions—a condition that frequently suggests purifying political action" (*DS*, 71). The attempt to bring spectators to a prepolitical frame of mind is most effective when conducted via a drama that is essentially a testimony of one's age (*testimonio*), given coherence and imaginative palpability by the author's own fictitious structure (*fábula*).

However, man's social circumstances are only one element of the world to be documented by the responsible dramatist, for Sastre's conception of that world is essentially existentialist. The fundamental realities to be revealed through the drama are those proper to human existence. The dramatic revelation of man's existential condition must be projected via concrete situations (sets of circumstances) in which fictional individuals find themselves, and man's social situation at a given moment is a conspicuous and changeable aspect of his total situation as an existing human being. The effect of a "social document" should therefore be transcendental: it should illuminate more general tragic realities of the human condition. Sastre's belief is that the realities revealed through the penetrative realism of testimonial theater are basic to human existence, and that the ultimate effect of documentation will be penetrating and disturbing, rather than merely photographic.

The foregoing notions, all of them relevant to Sastre's call for a theater of revelation and agitation, are captured and synthesized in his concept of tragedy. The development of a definition of tragedy is, indeed, the single major project undertaken in *Drama and Society*; the book's original section (Part I) is concerned entirely with this definition, as are several previously written essays included in Part II. Sastre's concern with tragedy dates from 1952; the subject's treatment in *Drama and Society* is, thus, a summary as well as an expansion of his thinking on it. In 1953 Sastre set forth a concise, though involved, definition of tragedy which, unfortunately, was not reproduced in *Drama and Society*:

> For me . . . tragedy is simply the dramatic (theatrical) result of the documentary transference of human existence to plots . . . that include painful events which provoke in those who suffer—or at least in the spectator—basic questions about the meaning of those events. Ultimately the questions concern human existence and the possibility of reducing, by means of human efforts, the effects of the painful events. The spectator participates in the anguish of the action, and through his grievous emotion—which consists of horror (*phobos*) and pity (*eleos*)—he may be moved to revise his view of the world and the assumptions of his life. He may be moved to make meaningful social decisions, ranging from individual assistance to revolution. When this happens, the tragedy has achieved its supreme end: purification (*katharsis*). Understood thus, purification consists of two stages: immediate or personal purification, and social purification.[20]

In this basic statement several elements stand out: an existentialist conception of tragedy, a vision of its agitating quality, a belief in its social effectiveness, and an adherence to Aristotelian concepts and terminology. These elements may be taken as an outline of Sastre's concept of tragedy in *Drama and Society*, and in years to come.

Sastre's reading of Aristotle's *Poetics* manifests itself in an interesting fusion with Sastre's modern sources. Sastre was quite aware of the extent to which the *Poetics* influenced the conception and composition of *Drama and Society*; in 1962, looking back on his first book, Sastre went so far as to say that his intention had been "merely to recall critically, and to modernize, the bases of Aristotle's *Poetics*."[21] This retrospective statement of intent differs somewhat from the one given in *Drama and Society*'s prologue, but it does not contradict it. Furthermore, it gives an essentially accurate idea of that book's first part and of its other essays which attempt to define and justify tragedy in the modern world. In his discussion of tragedy Sastre uses an Aristotelian terminology and he accepts Aristotle's notions of the tragedy's proper form. His total concept of tragedy is a fusion of these elements with existential and social concerns.

Sastre's attempt to update Aristotle's *Poetics* is based on a conviction that tragedy does still exist in the modern theater and that its form has remained essentially unchanged since Aristotle's time. The specific realities of a particular tragic situation may lose their relevancy with the passage of time because the theater is an essentially social art form: a dramatist writes for his contemporaries, and the failure or success of his work depends on the relationship established between the drama and its spectators. "Tragedy is something that functions in society. It is contaminated. It always serves a purpose. It may be useful or useless: it may enhance or obstruct social evolution—or revolution. It is in there functioning—among the things, among the institutions, forming part of the social dynamic" (*DS*, 55). This contemporary substance of a tragedy is corruptible; it is what gives the Greek classics a distant, foreign ring for the modern spectator (*DS*, 20). It is also the source of tragedy's potential effectiveness in bringing about a sharpening of consciences and an opposition to social injustice.[22]

On the other hand, tragedy consists also of another substance —a metaphysical substance—which does not lose its relevance with the passage of time. "Even if all social tragedies were eliminated, human existence would itself continue to be a great metaphysical tragedy" (*DS*, 138-39). This permanent, metaphysical substance is the source of the classical theater's enduring appeal; it is the link between *Oedipus Rex* and a "modern tragedy" such as O'Neill's *The Hairy Ape* or Miller's *Death of a Salesman.* The metaphysical substance of tragedy is, concisely, "human existence in its modality which Heidegger termed 'authentic'" (*DS*, 20). Thus, while a particular painful situation may eventually lose its power to move an audience, the tragedy's metaphysical substance transcends those situations and cuts across the distance between generations. "The tragic situation may . . . vanish. What does not vanish is the tragic nature of human existence in general. What does not change is human existence as we perceive it in the superstructures that it takes on in history" (*DS*, 37). The durable tragic quality of a particular drama "is proportional to the strength with which the theatrical situations refer back to (authentic) human existence in general . . ." (*DS*, 37).

It should be noted that Sastre insists on tragedy's reflection of human existence "in those rare moments when the farce of daily life melts away . . ." (*DS*, 23). He readily associates the concept with the thought of Heidegger and Unamuno (*DS*, 21), but he fails to mention Jean-Paul Sartre, whose influence is also quite clear in Sastre's delineation of human existence in its authentic modality. When the illusions of inauthentic existence are stripped away, human existence is a closed situation in which human beings, who are condemned to die, find themselves existing. Their primordial desire is to attain the happiness which is denied them; their failure to achieve happiness motivates them to wonder about their destiny, and about the anonymous sin or fault for which they are being punished. Human existence is a struggle in which the human being is always defeated; his failure provokes a horror of the catastrophe's magnitude and pity for the human project's defeat. The source of both these emotions is the fact of human existence (*DS*, 23-24).

The same existential conditions prominently and intensely characterize the tragic hero, and the same emotions are generated by his fate, whether he be Sophocles' Oedipus or O'Neill's Yank (*DS*, 24, 32). The tragedy thus becomes a "lucid representation of human existence" (*DS*, 33). It is the microcosmic image of man's agonizing contention with the eternal conditions of his existence, and with the particular circumstances of his historical moment.

Implicit in Sastre's existentialist vision of tragedy is the notion that the precise impulse which gives meaning to the tragedy is the human tendency to wonder about the meaning of human existence. More specifically, it is the mystery of the anonymous sin. On this point Sastre works from visible effect to presumed cause: man's suffering and death signify an eternal punishment —but at whose hands and for what transgression?[23] The mission of tragedy is to pry into this aspect of man's predicament. Communication with the spectator is established when tragedy at least illuminates the dilemma, or at best suggests an answer to the question posed. The primary query: Who or what is responsible for human suffering? is an essential part of Sastre's scale of dramatic values and of his own theater. The tragic genre defines itself for him by its investigational quality. However, since the human dilemma is two-pronged, so must be the investigation of it. Thus, the search for the guilty parties takes place at both the social and metaphysical levels.

The answers found at the metaphysical level can presumably lead only to a clarification of the human condition, to solidarity among the spectators, and to the cathartic effect of horror and pity. Such an illumination does not exactly place the blame for man's suffering and death, but it does clarify his possibilities by synthesizing his condition and illuminating his relations to the universe. Through its power to tear away the mist of painful confusion that characterizes man's daily life, tragedy can impel its spectators toward a reflection on their existence; such a frame of mind presumably affords a higher degree of satisfaction than does the forced, deceitful "happy ending" of non-tragic genres:[24] "Tragic exaltation makes human existence intelligible. . . . In the exaltation of the tragic event, a sense is suddenly brought to the grey, blurred mass of the cities, to human worries, human relations, work, recreation. The distortions of daily life suddenly disappear and everything falls into its proper place. That which appeared to be a dense, opaque reality . . . evaporates like a dream. The individual comes face to face with his true possibilities and only then can he say that he is happy: when he knows what to expect from destiny" (*DS*, 142-43).

Fear and pity, the principal emotions provoked in the spectator by the ideal tragedy, should lead to a personal purgation, or catharsis. The spectator voluntarily submits to the torture of the agonizing tragic spectacle because of a sense of personal guilt: he feels himself implicated in the suffering of all men, and he embraces torture and mortification as a cleansing experience. Sastre measures the degree of catharsis—and thus the effectiveness of a given tragedy—by the impact of the spectator's purgation on the reality of his circumstances: that is, the degree to which the spectator is moved to modify the painful conditions whose reflection he has just witnessed on the stage. The realities which he can and should be moved to modify are social conditions: the relations among human beings. A dramatist always writes for his contemporaries, according to Sastre, and the painful scenes he creates must relate to his historical moment (*DS*, 56). If he is an effective writer of tragedy, he will lead his audience to a reflection on the sources of human suffering; this reflection will ultimately inspire reparatory action, insofar as the sources of suffering are social and alterable (*DS*, 95). Thus, at the social level the effect of tragedy should be a tangible modification of the painful reality which originally inspired the work's composition. At the metaphysical or existential level its effect should be an illumination of the eternal conditions which will be the context of any social activity.

In order to accomplish these ends, a tragedy must agitate and disturb the conscience of its spectators, and Sastre makes formal demands on the dramatist which propose to fulfill this prime requirement. First, the tragedy should be constructed on a documentary base. It should be a composite of recognizable details of contemporary life which, when assembled on a fundamental plot structure, permit the desired catharsis and illumination in the spectator. Sastre regards "documentary theater" as the most vital feature of the twentieth-century drama; its roots are in Antoine's ultra-realism, but since the 1930's Antoine's detached documentation has been transcended by a realism which has an obviously agitating social intent. In Sinclair, Rice, Saroyan, Toller, Strich, Zückmayer, Brecht, Wilder, Sartre, and Miller the drama has rested on a strong base of details taken from contemporary life. In many plays by these dramatists the documentation has been used in such a way as to achieve the tragic impact. Miller's *Death of a Salesman* is one of Sastre's favorite examples of a modern documentary tragedy.[25]

Secondly, the tragic hero-victim must be "morally normal." Neither a saint nor a monster can be a tragic hero. The tragic situation must be one in which ". . . the men involved are always morally normal, for to the extent that there are 'good guys' and 'bad guys' the tragedy is undermined. And it should appear that those men are not really responsible for the painful situation in which they find themselves; . . . at most, they have committed an error, or an action that turns out to be an error because of its consequences" (*DS*, 27-28).

Although Sastre does not specify the standards to be used in determining the moral normality of the characters, one assumes that this quality is conceived with regard to the standards of the spectators for whom the tragic impact is intended. This consideration poses an obvious variable which must be resolved by resorting to myths general enough to capture the comprehension and empathy of a representative portion of the audience. If the characters are obviously evil and deserving of their fate, the disturbing tension in the drama—and consequently in the spectators—will not be realized. If the characters are saintly paragons of virtue, the tension is aborted in a different way: the tragic fate becomes inconceivable and can be effected only via sentimentalist melodrama.

This same tension is also implicit in a third quality which Sastre considers essential to tragedy: a multilateral portrayal of the conflict. This demand is a ramification of Sastre's basic aesthetic of agitation and his opposition to propagandist theater. The desirability of tension obviously discredits "thesis plays" in which a predetermined ideology, rather than documentation and plot, becomes the drama's starting point. "If the antagonist is also right, it is difficult to fire the revolutionary pistol at him" (*DS*, 49). The dramatist should exploit tragedy's social potential in good faith; rather than trying to win the audience to a particular political faction, he should strive only to stimulate the spectator's conscience and move him to a "prepolitical state" in which he will have an awareness of social injustice and an inclination to promote reparatory action (*DS*, 84). Tragedy's social projection should come through the purifying effect on the audience, rather than through brainwashing in support of a particular doctrine. The latter may be successful in inducing social change, but it is not tragedy because it does not achieve a synthesis of man's social and existential circumstances.

Fourthly, the tragic situation must be one from which there is no escape. The theoretical justification for this point is to be found once again in the vital importance of dramatic tension for Sastre. In this case the desired tension is that which exists between the character's efforts to overcome his fate, and the impossibility of doing so. The tragic situation does not have to be unchangeable in an absolute way; it is sufficient that there be no possible escape for the hero within the given circumstances of the play. The social circumstances within which the drama unfolds can, in fact, presumably be changed. Their modification through the years is one source of the gap between an ancient tragedy and the modern spectator. But the tragedy is written primarily for an audience of contemporaries, and its impact on that audience depends on its success in presenting situations from which there is no escape in terms of present realities (*DS*, 36).[26] Furthermore, it should be remembered that one of tragedy's significant possibilities is that of inspiring the spectator to seek solutions to the problems and injustices reflected in the drama. In order to have this effect the tragic situation would have to be one from which there is no escape, but from which there could be an escape (at the social level) if certain conditions were altered.

It becomes increasingly evident that Sastre's "modernization" of Aristotle's *Poetics* consists of the addition of a social function which Aristotle did not regard as proper to tragedy. Aristotle "accepted . . . the Greek notion that the fine arts have no end beyond themselves."[27] Furthermore, he saw the desired effect of tragedy's purgation as that of "reconciling us to our fate, because we understand it as the universal human lot."[28] Sastre, as we have seen, insists that tragedy should promote discontent rather than reconciliation, and he considers the effective tragedy to be one that produces tangible repercussions outside the theater. Aristotle suggests that tragedy springs from two basic instincts of human nature: man's instinct to imitate, and his natural desire for rhythm and harmony.[29] Sastre's existentialism leads him to seek tragedy's origin in man's tendency to wonder about the reasons for his condition.

In other respects, however, Sastre has adhered to Aristotelian notions of tragedy. Aristotle alternately defines tragedy as an imitation of men in action, "an imitation of an action that is serious, complete, and of a certain magnitude . . ." and an imitation of "actions which excite pity and fear."[30] His insistence on tragedy's imitation of action might seem to differ from Sastre's concept of tragedy as a revelatory image of man's existential and social circumstances. The divergence, however, is only apparent. When one understands Aristotle's concept of action, it becomes obvious that Sastre's existentialism has not really led him to a radically different definition of tragedy. By "action" Aristotle does not mean physical activity, "but a movement-of-spirit, and by 'imitation' he means, not superficial copying, but the representation of the countless forms which the life of the human spirit may take. . . ."[31] Action (*praxis*) is not the deeds or events themselves, but rather the motivation from which they spring. "The *praxis* that art seeks to reproduce is mainly a psychic energy working outwards."[32] In the light of this more sophisticated conception one can indeed see an Aristotelian "action" at the heart of Sastre's ideal tragedy.

In the same way Sastre's existentialist concept of tragedy embraces the Aristotelian notion that tragedy (poetry) should express that which is common to all men: "Poetry . . . is a more philosophical and a higher thing than history: for poetry tends to express the universal, history the particular."[33] Universality will be attained only if the actions imitated are characterized by "the grave and the constant."[34] In Sastre's dichotomy between the tragedy's "metaphysical" and "social" substances, the former would certainly be "universal" as well as "grave and constant." The social substance of tragedy, and the documentation upon which it depends, would seem to be censured in Aristotle's statement that ". . . it is not the function of the poet to relate what has happened, but what may happen—what is possible according to the laws of probability or necessity."[35] On the basis of this statement one would assume that Aristotle would consider Sastre's "documentation" more proper to the historian than to the writer of tragedy. Once again, however, a seemingly un-Aristotelian concept exposed in *Drama and Society* could conceivably be justified in relation to the *Poetics*, for Aristotle does authorize some modes of journalistic documentation in the tragedy: ". . . the poet or 'maker' should be the maker of plots rather than of verses, since he is a poet because he imitates, and what he imitates are actions. And even if he chances to take an historical subject, he is none the less a poet; for there is no reason why some events that have actually happened should not conform to the law of the probable and possible, and in virtue of that quality in them he is their poet or maker."[36] In other words, documentation as Sastre conceives it would appear to be permitted, so long as it has a value which transcends the anecdote of the particular circumstances in which it has its origin. Such is, indeed, the potential which Sastre attributes to tragic documentation.

Perhaps the most basic and most lasting contribution of the *Poetics* to Sastre's thought was that it left him with a firm respect for unity and primacy of plot in a drama's construction. Aristotle's evaluation of plot ("the arrangement of the incidents") as "the first principle, and, as it were, the soul of a tragedy . . ." derives from his conception of tragedy as the imitation of an action: a single, unified action.[37] Tragedy does not imitate men or ideas, but an action, and that action finds its dramatic reality in the plot. With his ever-present concern for the impact on the spectator, Aristotle recalls, furthermore, that the plot is the vehicle for the two most powerful appeals to the spectator's emotions: Reversal and Recognition. A single action has a more concentrated effect on the spectator, and a single action signifies a unified plot.

Sastre's concern for the principles of unity, equilibrium, and primacy of plot certainly has a less elaborate theoretical framework, but it is essential to, and consistent with, the rest of his thought. First, he rejects the neoclassical insistence on three unities and defends the Aristotelian concept of one single unity (*DS*, 41). Secondly, he insists—as does Aristotle—that the plot should be the source of all other elements of the drama: "Whenever the importance of the plot has been slighted, the result has always been dramatic monstrosities" (*DS*, 45). Sastre's theoretical justification for these principles lies in his frequently expressed concern for the effect of the drama on the spectator and, through the spectator, on the world. This effect is dependent upon a tension to which the spectator must be subjected: "Tragic *exaltation* on the stage produces tragic *tension* in the spectator . . ." (*DS*, 143).[38] Tension implies polarity and equilibrium, which are achieved through a dramatic structure whose foundation is precisely an ordered collection of incidents pertinent to one basic movement, or action in the Aristotelian sense. If some element other than the plot—for example, a political doctrine or the characters' psychological quirks—were the drama's starting point, the action would be subordinated to that element and the vital tension would be aborted. "The dramatist, swayed by his sympathy for the political ideas of the protagonist and his hostility toward those of the antagonist, either refuses to let the antagonist speak, or else he has him speak in a stupid, cruel or inhuman manner. The drama loses strength, the plot turns out forced, and the characters are weakened. This is the general danger of 'thesis' theater. The dramatist clings to his thesis, chokes off the antithesis, and naturally ends up a long way from a dramatic synthesis" (*DS*, 118-19).

The "dramatic synthesis," then, is the aesthetic ideal of *Drama and Society*. Considered variously as presumed cause or desired effect, the concept underlies Sastre's principles of revelation, agitation, tension, equilibrium, and penetrative realism, as well as his formulistic structural requirements for the tragedy. One may question Sastre's suggestion that all these elements add up to "modern tragedy"; one of the major weaknesses of *Drama and Society* is surely Sastre's rather simplistic application of the term "tragedy" to plays so diverse as those he constantly cites: *Death of a Salesman, The Hairy Ape, The Dirty Hands, No Exit,* and the German Expressionist theater. His terminology would perhaps have proven more consistent had he simply adhered to the implications of his book's title and outlined the requirements for a socially effective "drama." Regardless of the terminology, however, one must recognize a certain coherence in *Drama and Society*. Sastre has defined and explored what he considers the most relevant kind of theater. His aesthetic values are fundamentally Aristotelian and are stamped with characteristic twentieth-century existentialism and social leftism. It would be hazardous, as well as pointless, to speculate as to which aspect of Sastre's thought—the influence of Aristotle or social leftism—crystallized first. The significant fact is that *Drama and Society* represents a fusion of the two—a relating of aesthetic theories to social convictions. That same fusion, in varying forms, continues to be characteristic of Sastre's thought in succeeding essays and in his second book, *Anatomía del realismo* (*Anatomy of Realism*).

CHAPTER 3

The Later Essays

I *Intellectual Evolution After* Drama and Society

ALFONSO Sastre's thought undergoes no radical reversals in the years following *Drama and Society*. His essays of the eight years which follow his first book's publication continue to reveal Sastre's existentialist point of departure, as well as his parallel concern for man's situation as a social creature. His exigencies for the drama continue to be essentially those presented in *Drama and Society*: the relevant drama must agitate and illuminate, at both the existential and social levels.

This continuation of Sastre's early themes, however, should not be interpreted as intellectual stagnation, for there is definitely evolution within the basic continuing framework. The principles previously enunciated in *Drama and Society* become more clearly defined. Sastre now tends to articulate his convictions in terms of their relation to specific realities rather than in the general and often confusing notions of that early book. Moreover, one notes a more mature conception of the interrelation among the various principles at stake—notably existentialism and social responsibility—as well as a more delicate sense of their relative significance.

Sastre's existentialism as set forth in *Drama and Society* had been a general, somewhat superficial paraphrasing of Sartre and Heidegger. During the second major phase of Sastre's ideological development that vision becomes sharper and more tightly related to its aesthetic and social ramifications. The existentialist doctrine of human existence as the point of departure for all reality is suggested in Sastre's review of the book *The Theater in Life*, by Nikolai Evreinov. Sastre vigorously rejects Evreinov's suggestion that the theater is endowed with a metaphysical primacy and that human life is essentially theater, or an imitation of theater: "Evreinov tells us that theater is the origin, the meaning, and the substance of life. The truth of the matter is, in fact, just the opposite: the origin, meaning, and substance of theater must be sought in life. Man first 'finds himself' living and then comes everything else—including theater. One cannot say that man 'finds himself' involved in theater and that this activity constitutes his life."[1] This statement is an obvious embodiment of the Existentialist commonplace, "Existence precedes essence." It is also an attempt by Sastre to lend philosophical support to his basic assertions regarding the theater's function as investigation and representation of human life: "Theater consists of a representation, and even an investigation, of life, and it mimetically adopts the forms of the life which it attempts to represent."[2]

Another index of Sastre's persistent existentialism, and of his tendency to relate this abstract thought to specific literary interests, is his reaction to Samuel Beckett's *Waiting for Godot* between 1957 and 1965. This play was introduced to Madrid's theater public by the Pequeño Teatro Dido on March 28, 1956. In April, 1957, the text of *Waiting for Godot* was published in Spanish in the first issue of *Primer acto,* along with Sastre's first study of that play.[3] This essay is undoubtedly one of Sastre's most perceptive pieces of literary criticism even though he later rejects some of its statements and suggestions.

In this study Sastre lucidly presents *Waiting for Godot* as a dramatic representation of man's existential situation, and in so doing he naturally reveals much of his own vision: "*Waiting for Godot* captures perfectly that series of non-events that makes up our daily existence. This is why the picture it presents is a familiar one—an X-ray in which we recognize ourselves with horror. The plot of *Waiting for Godot* is nothing more nor less than the plot of our life."[4]

Human incommunication, the ontological gulf that separates man from himself, man's tortured and futile longing for a realm of being where that separation does not exist, the relentless and ironic presence of death, which reduces all human projects to self-deluding games: the entire human predicament, as outlined in general terms in *Drama and Society,* is apparent to Sastre in Beckett's tragicomedy. Sastre sees the pointless waiting of the play's characters as the representation of humanity's hopeful wait for a salvation that never comes:

Waiting for Godot is many things: a sorrowful moan at twilight, a last will and testament, an announcement of the coming end, a letter to the coroner, a cry for help in the night, a funeral song. *Waiting for Godot* is a death certificate that bears the name "Hope." We shall continue to show up for our appointment under the tree alternately barren and green. We shall continue to fight off our desperate boredom with games, words, hunger, thoughts of suicide. But from now on we know that Godot will not keep the appointment. We shall continue to wait, but our wait will now be a wait without hope.[5]

Sastre's lyrical "epitaph" for Vladimir and Estragon is a résumé of the human condition which he sees reflected in Beckett's play:

They were sad that evening when they died. They had come for their appointment, as usual, there by the tree, and they felt more alone than ever. A cold wind was blowing. And no one came. They weren't sure they had the right place, but there was nowhere else they could wait. They looked at each other for a moment and then wept bitterly, with a grief that was a summing-up of their existence. They separated forever, each going his own way. They died, of cold and loneliness. As they died they cried out. And then the world was quiet again.[6]

One senses that Sastre was profoundly and irrevocably impressed by *Waiting for Godot,* and that this essay of 1957 was the result of that play's initial impact on him. This circumstance was a fortunate one from the reader's standpoint, for it probably accounts for the essay's lyricism and spontaneity—qualities which are often lacking in Sastre's more meditated, cerebral efforts. Later, however, Sastre was predictably bothered by the implicit nihilism of *Waiting for Godot* and of his own reaction to it. The basic tension of Sastre's intellectual life has been a struggle against nihilism; his initial and later reactions to *Waiting for Godot* exemplify this struggle. Viewing the total range of Sastre's writings on *Waiting for Godot* from 1957 to 1965, one sees that his feelings toward the play are mixed and often contradictory. The inconsistency of his reaction seems to stem from Sastre's own fear that he will take Beckett's theater too seriously. He has great admiration for Beckett, but he has declared, "It would horrify me to be the author of *Waiting for Godot.*"[7]

It is significant that Sastre is horrified by something which he also respects and to which he is drawn. He admires and is moved by Beckett's play because it confirms his own propensity to view man in terms of his existential predicament, but his resistance to its nihilistic temptations parallels the other major dimension of Sastre's thought: the necessity to transcend the existential condition via meaningful action. Thus, Sastre's dual attitude toward *Waiting for Godot* is actually his old contradiction posed in new terms. The opposition of liberty versus commitment, so obvious in Sastre's early years, now assumes the form of existential anguish, with its nihilistic temptations, versus existential transcendence in the form of meaningful action.

"Meaningful action," for Sastre, is social activity, and this is the alternative which he opposes to existential anguish in his later comments on *Waiting for Godot*. While he never explicitly denounces this play, neither does he ever again abandon himself to the subjectivity that characterized his first essay. He continues to respect Beckett as a playwright, but at the same time he presents Beckett's avant-garde world as something to be overcome. As Sastre tends increasingly toward Marxism as a possible means of opposing the agonizing human incommunication represented in the Theater of the Absurd, he brands Beckett's theater as an anti-historical representation of man: ". . . it is a theater of concrete existence: a theater of suffering, of the absurd, of incommunication, of immanence, and of death."[8] He contrasts this theater with that of Bertolt Brecht, which presents man as history, rather than as pure existence: ". . . in [Brecht's] theater, man is an historical subject, the object of progressive transformation . . ."[9] Sastre makes no explicit value judgment between the two images of man, but his preference for the latter is clearly implied. Both the theater of Beckett and that of Brecht, Sastre suggests, are convincing, but the anti-historical theater presents man in an untranscendental mode and consequently offers no stimulus to seek the future.

In a footnote appended to a later edition of his first essay on *Waiting for Godot*, Sastre again makes reference to that play's anti-historical perspective, and he reveals the evolution of his own attitude by interpreting a comment he had previously made in that first essay. In explanation of his earlier assertion that the plot of *Waiting for Godot* was "the plot of our life," Sastre writes: "We must not see this as a nihilistic assertion . . . but rather as a polemical, socio-historical postulate. I am referring here to the problem of 'alienation.' The same could be said of the 'schism of the human being.' "[10] The implication of this later observation is that *Waiting for Godot* represents human life as it is, but not as it must be. The agonizing alienation projected by that play is viewed as the consequence of human history and as a symptom of the modern crisis of the bourgeoisie. Thus, while not actually contradicting his earlier observations, Sastre retrospecively interprets them in the light of socialist principles formulated chronologically between the two publications of that first essay.

Sastre's most recent written pronouncement on Beckett appears to have been made in 1965. He now includes Beckett's "nihilistic tragicomedy" as one of several dubious genres which populate a theatrical world unfortunately deficient in relevant social tragedy.[11] Thus the trajectory of Sastre's expressed attitude toward Beckett goes from an initial subjective identification with *Waiting for Godot* to an ultimate resistance to Beckett's allure. The evolution of this particular attitude is only one feature of the more general evolution of Sastre's thought. In 1960 he had written: ". . . my evolution is taking me from an extreme, rebellious spiritualism toward a spiritualism of a more materialist, revolutionary nature."[12] On the basis of Sastre's essays of the late 1950's and early 1960's, one can only agree with his appraisal of his own intellectual evolution. The existentialist-socialist duality is a constant of Sastre's intellectual framework, but it is undeniable that since approximately 1960 he has placed primary emphasis on man in his social mode. An increasingly intransigent Marxism, it would seem, has been the ultimate ideological stance of a man who has avoided despair only by tenaciously resisting his immediate inclinations. The evolution is not a linear one; in Sastre's later essays, as well as in his theater, the anguish of life's futility occasionally regains its dominance over the humanistic emphasis on life's purpose. But the trend is clear.

Social revolution emerges as Sastre's favorite concrete symbol of the humanistic task at hand. Revolutionary themes are a prominent feature of Sastre's theater; his essays which deal with the revolution as social reality and as dramatic device are, in general, clarifications of his own theater. Sastre does not present revolution as a glorious and automatic salvation of oppressed humanity, but rather as "a tragic reality . . . a great sacrifice . . . often a bloodbath."[13] Whatever naïveté Sastre may have shown on this subject in *Drama and Society* has disappeared in his later writings on social revolution. He realizes, in part as early as 1957, that social change brought about by force is a painful process which is itself a tragedy. It must be endured, however, if social injustice —which is even more unacceptable—is to be overcome: ". . . it may be true that every revolution is a tragic event, but every unjust social order is also a tragedy: a muted, unacceptable tragedy. I attempt to place the spectator before the dilemma of choosing between these two tragedies. It is true that the silent tragedy of the unjust social order can be destroyed only by the tragedy of a revolution. The hope lies in a positive outcome of this second tragedy, which is, or should be, shrill and open, as compared to the stifled, chronic, closed nature of the other one."[14]

Every individual involved in the tragedy of revolution will feel its painful effects, but the conflict is especially difficult for the intellectual. A revolution is a violent and sometimes arbitrary implantation of a new order whose only justification is the hope that it will bring a greater degree of social justice than did its predecessor. Long-range humanistic values must take precedence over fear and reluctance if the revolution is to succeed. But those values are embodied in a possibility, rather than a reality, and the revolutionary intellectual finds his moral scruples and analytical tendencies sacrificed on behalf of a dogmatism which may ultimately produce a better society, but which immediately is distasteful to any thinking, sensitive human being. Sastre regards such a dilemma as inevitable for a leftist intellectual, and by 1962 he had begun to articulate this conflict as a theoretical background for the socially conscious writer: "This whole series of problems forms part of what has been called the 'intellectual schism,' produced by a conflict which, although still quite real, will gradually disappear. I refer to the conflict between thinking individuals and collective movements, between ethics and politics, reflection and activism, liberty and necessity."[15]

The revolutionary writer thus has a choice between two possible stances: he may give himself to the dogmatism of a cause, or he may strive to retain his intellectual integrity by portraying the revolution as conflict, rather than as absolute dogma. It is hardly surprising that Sastre has more respect for the second attitude, or that it is the principle which continues to govern his own literary production. His preference for agitation over dogmatism carries with it the problem of ambiguity in the works and misinterpretation by the public, but he prefers this problem to the intellectual prostitution of "party literature": ". . . with varying degrees of success, I try to avoid writing literature that is infantile, one-sided, and simplistic."[16] Sastre's rejection of unilateral literature persists, but his revolutionary inclinations have grown stronger during the six years since *Drama and Society*. The resultant conflict is but another facet of his intellectual dualism, the tension of which provides the dramatic strength of his own plays.

It is interesting that Sastre predicts the eventual end of the conflicts between individual integrity and efforts to build a better world. He sees their present existence as symptomatic of a fragmented humanity; the conflicts, thus, will disappear before the unity of a new humanism: "I believe they will disappear as a new humanism crystallizes in our society. This is, for me, the movement of history."[17] This growing humanistic optimism is a clear characteristic of Sastre's intellectual evolution during the years between his two books. His writings of this period suggest a recurring difficulty in maintaining that posture—a difficulty which, as we have repeatedly observed, produces the intellectual tension so characteristic of Sastre's thought. His optimism is the future-oriented attitude which he himself encourages as a prime value for the theater: an historical vision of man's material efforts to create a better world, and a faith in the possibility of achieving this end through united human action. A prerequisite for the new order is the eradication of the old one, and this step, in turn, depends upon a clarification of contemporary injustices. For Sastre, this illumination, via a theater of agitation, continues to be the ultimate justification of drama in the modern world.

II *The Search for Form: Tragedy and Realism*

The many directions from which Alfonso Sastre approaches the problem of dramatic form in *Drama and Society* are gradually condensed into two basic principles: tragedy and realism. These had already been the keys to Sastre's theoretical groping in his first book, including, as they did, such subordinate notions as *realismo profundizado, social-realismo, teatro testimonial, teatro existencial,* and *teatro de angustia.* Now, in the years before publication of *Anatomy of Realism,* tragedy and realism emerge as the explicit theoretical bases of Sastre's continuing search for effective dramatic form.

Both these principles are summaries of Sastre's previous attitudes, but the summaries are colored by an expanding vision of the principles and of their relation to a general conception of the drama. Tragedy continues to be defined as a synthesis of the ways in which vital appeals can be made to man: "pathetically, a lament for the hero's death; ontologically, a representation of reality; existentially, an authentic situation; ethically, a criminal investigation; socially, a public accusation; politically, a purifying operation; religiously, a collective sacrifice; ideologically, a form of knowledge; psychologically, a world in liberty; aesthetically, a dramatic form—but above all, a song of hope . . ."[18]

There is, however, a certain shift in the perspective with which Sastre discusses the tragic genre during his second period. Tragedy is now conceived precisely as a "song of hope" embodied in a transcendence of both the optimism and the pessimism which are frequently considered tragedy's prime characteristics. In relation to tragedy, the term "optimism" has a rather special connotation for Sastre. By optimism he means the falsely favorable image of domestic social conditions which a government invariably tries to present to its citizens. The responsible dramatist must oppose this "bureaucratic optimism," since the theater's mission is to disturb rather than to placate. Tragedy, as Sastre conceives it, is the theatrical genre which by its very nature presents an opposition to official social optimism.

On the other hand, the "pessimism" which tragedy must also avoid is not social, but existential. Thus, while denying the existence of optimum social conditions, the writer of tragedy must also avoid any suggestion of nihilistic futility. He must portray man's existential condition, but only in light of the possibility of combating it. The dualism of Sastre's tragic vision thus reappears in an explicit form: ". . . in its most perfect forms, tragedy implies a dialectical transcendence of pessimism (usually deriving from existential concerns) and optimism (usually deriving from social concerns) . . ."[19]

The two extremes of optimistic social naïveté and gloomy existential despair are thus rejected as equally pernicious for the tragedy. Both are antidialectical, and therefore oppressive, outlooks. Tragedy fuses them into a constructive dialectic in which man's individual and social lives create a dramatic tension. Sastre's insistence on this synthesis, here and elsewhere, is a summary of his reservations about Beckett's theater, his existentialist-socialist dualism, and the intellectual tension which he translates into dramatic theory.

Sastre continues to insist on "realism" as the theater's only valid mode. This insistence is a logical correlative to his definition of tragedy, both in *Drama and Society* and later. However, just as Sastre's perspective of tragedy is modified in his second period, so do his notions of realism become more liberal and more sophisticated. In *Drama and Society* Sastre had placed great emphasis on the documentary heritage of twentieth-century theater. He had pointed to Antoine as the fountainhead of all modern realism and had maintained that documentation of man's existence must be the starting point for relevant theater. After 1956, as Sastre dedicates increasing attention to the problems of realism in the theater, he moves away from his insistence on a documentary point of departure and toward a tolerance of many dramatic styles quite removed from the imitative intent of Antoine.[20]

The belief that human reality is complex, and that its artistic representation can take many different forms, was the principle on which Sastre and Quinto founded the Grupo de Teatro Realista in 1960. The theoretical base of this group was precisely an admission that realism in the theater takes many forms, all of which merit consideration: ". . . the G.T.R. has not employed the term 'realism' in order that it be gratuitously accepted, but rather in the hope that it will be discussed. We do not aspire to impose a dogma, but simply to make a proposal."[21] The group's liberal policy of programing, however, pertained to the style and form of the plays to be performed. Its ideology was a continuation of Sastre's earlier principles of socially responsible theater: "a theater which is the dramatic result of serious, meaningful encounters between the dramatist and his existential circumstance. We will stage these plays with an awareness of our situation and with an intent to have an impact—on the Spanish theater, as well as . . . on the social process of which we are a part."[22]

The liberalization of Sastre's concept of realism gives his dramatic theories a broader scope, but it also implies certain theoretical problems. *Drama and Society*, although hindered by contradictions and a ratheir naïve vision, had a least been quite explicit in its definition of realism. Sastre had undoubtedly misrepresented the importance of Antoine's documentary legacy, but the exigencies which he derived from that original premise were reasonably clear and convincing. With the weakening of Sastre's insistence on documentation as the basis of modern realism, the term *realismo* grows vague. The lessening of Sastre's dogmatism on this point, and his increasingly mature awareness of the subtleties of human experience, are reflected in the confusion and contradictions of his essays in the late 1950's and 1960's. In the face of such a general admission of "realistic" styles, Sastre's reader concludes that virtually every form of theater is acceptably "realistic" since very play touches some aspect of human reality. In his rejection of the imitative concept of realism, Sastre goes to the opposite extreme. In so doing he weakens whatever convincing quality there might have been in his earlier theoretical dogma. He appears to reject the foundations of his previous theoretical structure before clearly defining their replacements. The result is that his essays of this period, although more subtle and more interesting than his earlier writings, lack a solid theoretical unity.

Sastre appears to have been aware of the danger that an acceptance of many different forms of realism would render the term and concept meaningless. The G.T.R. had been founded on a liberal conception of realism: "authors carelessly labeled by some as 'non-realists' should not think themselves excluded . . . for our concept of realism is a broad one, and the G.T.R. is by no means intended as a vehicle for naturalism . . ."[23] Later, however, Sastre felt obliged to ask and answer an obvious question concerning the group's ideology and intent: ". . . its repertory will not be determined on the basis of any particular dogma. On the contrary, it will consist of a variety of forms.

Does that mean that the group could have been called simply 'Theater Group'"?[24] Sastre's answer to this question is, of course, negative. He draws a distinction between the "realistic theater" proposed by the G.T.R., and the "escapist, inhibitory theater" so prevalent in Spain. The ultimate aim which he enunciates for the G.T.R. coincides with his own criteria for effective drama: "may the spectator become generally aware of his existential situation, and specifically aware of his historical situation."[25] But although this declaration is consistent with Sastre's earlier ideals, it does not answer the basic question: What is realism? Neither is the question resolved by the vague reference to realism's supposed opposite, "escapist, inhibitory theater." Thus, the G.T.R., like many of Sastre's essays of this period, appears to have been conceived as a means of exploring a basic theoretical dilemma of which Sastre was aware, although not always admittedly so.

A major source of Sastre's confusion on the question of realism during these years was clearly his existentialism. Just as he came to restrain his enthusiasm toward *Waiting for Godot* because this play showed only one facet of man's dual condition as a social and existential creature, so Sastre seems to have liberalized his definition of realism for the same reason. He still regarded the theater as "a testimony of the world in which we live, or rather, of our being-in-the-world . . ."[26] Envisioned thus, the dramatist's testimony would supposedly include a reflection of man's social and existential circumstances. Sastre had outlined this same dual perspective in *Drama and Society*, but he had simultaneously tended to undermine his own theoretical structure. He had insisted that modern "tragedy" be cast in the photographic, documentary tradition of Antoine, apparently overlooking the fact that it is patently difficult to "document" metaphysical pressures in this fashion. Thus, despite his theoretical dualism, Sastre had prescribed essentially a theater of social protest. Realizing, consciously or otherwise, that he had slighted one term of his intended duality, he reacted by recognizing "realism" in plays which would not have fit his earlier formulas.

Sastre's first essay on *Waiting for Godot* again serves as a convenient example. Somewhat self-consciously, he insists that Beckett's play is, despite opinions to the contrary, a realistic work.

It is, according to Sastre, a vital, meaningful synthesis of previous movements whose intent had been, paradoxically, escapist:

> I have never seen a more realistic or less fantastic drama. . . . The problem is that the term "realism" is normally used with reference to only one of its forms: Naturalism—the superficial realism, the photographic testimony cultivated by Antoine for the *Théâtre Libre*. But the term actually has other meanings as well. I have called attention elsewhere to the existence of a "penetrative" tendency which has made possible the complex forms of a penetrative realism in the literature and art of our time. That process was nourished . . . by the experiments of movements which aspired to be anti-realist. All those "isms" have contributed to the development of realism.[27]

One can hardly doubt that Sastre's enthusiastic recognition of *Waiting for Godot* as a "realistic" play is the antithetical reaction to his earlier emphasis on documentation as the prime quality of realism. He goes on to compare the realism of *Waiting for Godot* to that of an X-ray: the image projected is not immediately recognizable like that of a snapshot, but it is much more profound. The comparison is interesting. It suggests, however, that the play's relevancy lies in its metaphysics. If this is true, *Waiting for Godot* does not achieve the synthesis of man's historical and existential pressures, so strongly advocated by Sastre.

Another example of Sastre's defense of non-photographic realism is his evaluation of his own collection of stories, *Las noches lúgubres* (*Lugubrious Nights*). Apparently fearing he would be accused of indulging in irrelevant fantasies, Sastre attempted to justify his stories in terms of their realism. These stories portray, he maintained, certain aspects "*of reality*, or of characters who are really *phantasmagoric* and menacing, either from our own world or from the realm of delirium and halucination. Because they are not immediately recognizable, these phenomena might appear to be unreal, but in fact they are just as real as those that found their way into the old 'realism' . . ."[28]

Few would argue that existential anguish and psychic torment are divorced from human reality, or that relevant and effective literature cannot be written on these themes. Indeed, Sastre is not the only critic to be impressed by the terrifying realism of Beckett's theater.[29] The weakness of Sastre's approach to realism during this period lies not in his intuitions, but rather in his rationalization of these intuitions. One suspects that Sastre's concept of realism could actually be delineated quite simply, for behind his theoretical confusion realism appears as that quality which renders a work of art relevant and complete. His deficient articulation of this concept is due largely to his insistence on the existentialist-socialist framework for his probing. The fundamental implication of Sastre's theoretical writings is that the ideal realism would be a synthesis of these two perspectives of human life. His own definitions and examples of realism however, tend to vacillate from thesis to antithesis. Sastre's second book, *Anatomy of Realism,* is essentially an intensification of the search for synthesis.

III Anatomía del realismo (Anatomy of Realism)

The reader of Sastre's *Anatomy of Realism* will probably be bothered by the book's obscure style before he is impressed by its intellectual penetration. For example:

> Critical, transitionary realism will continue to appear frequently as testimony of the oppositions (antagonistic or otherwise) between "existentialist" literature and "socialist" literature; and a broad horizon seems to be opening up in the form of a "dialectical realism" (profound and all-inclusive), capable of offering the most profound "reflection" of present reality, capable of constituting (creating) the most expressive myths for our historical moment and fulfilling a prophetic mission in an area which only in a limited sense could be assimilated into the (habitually infraliterary) field of "Science Fiction"; a field in which it will surely integrate the world of the dreams and illusions (and terrors!) of men, perhaps in the form of an improved romanticism.[30]

Such passages are not uncommon in *Anatomy of Realism.* This tortured prose style is accompanied by frequent contradictory or hybrid phrases which make the reader's task even more difficult: "active contemplation," "disinterested interest," "is-and-is-not," "takes-robs-assumes" (*AR,* 211, 213, 201, 191). Moreover, in this book Sastre is prone to conceptual contradiction and is often reluctant to make categorical affirmations. After a lengthy discourse on the dialectical character of realism, he concludes: ". . . it appears obvious that we would consider 'realistic' only that literature which offers a dialectical image of the world. However, such is not the case" (*AR*, 124-25). Sastre offers a detailed rejection of the polemic which opposes "art for art's sake" and "utilitarian" art; then he immediately detects a possible weakness in his argument: "I have denied . . . the contemporary validity of the 'utilitarianism—art-for-art's-sake' polemic; but now I may be criticized for having chosen the most obvious argument . . . instead of using terms more acceptable to the world's intelligentsia" (*AR*, 182). The hesitant or contradictory quality of other examples is self-evident: "On the other hand, in art the imaginary is the least real and the most true of all" (*AR*, 201); "I begin by confronting this question: What is happening in today's theater? But I no sooner define this problem than I am assaulted by a doubt . . ." (*AR*, 209).

In short, *Anatomy of Realism* is not an easy book to read and its ideas are not easily grasped. It would be quite unjust, however, to dismiss this collection of essays as pedantry or obscurantism. Its annoying labyrinth of contradiction is due, paradoxically, to its positive attribute. In *Anatomy of Realism* Sastre attempts to move toward an ultimate definition of realism via a formal dialectical method of argumentation. Such a method is a natural consequence of his earlier obsession for analysis, his insistence on trial and error, his attempts to synthesize opposing patterns of thought or conduct. A method of contradictory argumentation is now employed in an attempt to find a median point between contradictory principles. The written exposition of such a procedure will inevitably involve conceptual and semantic contradictions, as well as stylistic density.

One may ask, of course, how much of *Anatomy of Realism* is sound dialectical argumentation and how much is simply unfounded confusion. There is, indeed, some of the latter—in the concepts, in their treatment, and in the very structure of the book. One suspects that *Anatomy of Realism*, in order to become a cogent unity, would have to be edited and modified by someone other than its author, for the relentless dialectical workings of Sastre's mind appear by now to have disposed him against the omission of any detail which might contribute a bit of additional light to a given analysis, but which frequently serves only to cloud the basic issues. Despite the book's ineffective presentation, however, a reader can render a just evaluation only by recognizing Sastre's dialectical intent and by regarding his method as a natural vehicle for the concepts conveyed.

In its composition, *Anatomy of Realism* parallels Sastre's first book, *Drama and Society,* in that it includes previously published essays as well as some original material. The volume was published in 1965, but its essays date from as early as 1957 and deal with many of Sastre's favorite topics: social responsibility of the artist, problems of the theater in Spain, the G.T.R., tragedy, realism, Beckett, and Brecht. As in *Drama and Society* the essays' titles have generally been altered "in order to reflect the criteria for the selection and arrangement of these essays" (*AR,* 15). The material published for the first time in *Anatomy of Realism* includes essays written specifically for inclusion in this volume, essays originally intended for publication elsewhere, and alterations in the text of some previously published items. In addition there is an appendix which contains two very recent essays, written and published in magazines after the original manuscript of *Anatomy of Realism* was completed, but before the book was actually published.

As he did with *Drama and Society,* Sastre defends his second book's loose structure by declaring, *a priori,* that it was not his intention to write a systematic treatise, but rather to assemble the testimony of a writer whose discoveries relate to the concrete situation in which they have been made: ". . . the idea . . . is to present the theme of literary realism as it has manifested itself, through its many problems, to a dramatist who . . . has never resigned himself to not understanding the material of his existence and the real structure of his literary activity . . . in society in general, and in the Spanish situation in particular. So I have gathered here the work and the life of a writer, and the result is a bit of intellectual biography as well as an essay which has more the structure of life itself than that of a learned and systematic treatise" (*AR,* 8). In this comment—both explanation and self-defense—taken from the book's preface, one sees already Sastre's dialectical vision as it applies to his second book, to his own life, and to the relation between the two. *Anatomy of Realism* is, indeed, a sort of intellectual autobiography of its author, and in it the reader perceives Sastre's attempts to reflect the vital process of his own life: the process of experimentation, negation, and renewal. In this book Sastre insistently calls attention to the importance of his practical literary and theatrical activities in the formulation of his theories. His life, like his thought, has moved on parallel impulses which tug at each other, each seeking fallacies in the other, and both seeking a median point of reconciliation. On a higher level, both his life and his thought, taken as totalities, have polarized themselves in relation to certain concrete realities of contemporary Spain. Essential features of *Anatomy of Realism,* then, are its internal tension and its antagonistic attitude toward oppressive social structures and toward literary forms which tend to perpetuate those structures.

A specific phase of his past experience which Sastre aspires to negate with his second book is *Drama and Society*. The preface to *Anatomy of Realism,* written seven years after the publication of *Drama and Society,* is dedicated largely to an evaluation of the latter; it suggests that Sastre would like to negate his earlier work and that part of himself which was represented therein. He briefly points to some of his first book's errors—which, of course, have become "errors" only by virtue of Sastre's retrospective point of view. His recently acquired familiarity with Brecht leads him to conclude that *Drama and Society* was, from its very inception, "an anachronistic book": it had aspired to relate Aristotelian principles to the needs of the modern world, but Brecht had already "related" them by denying their validity. In 1963 Sastre sees that the value of *Drama and Society* was diminished by the absence of any consideration of Brecht, whose theories of the drama had been current in the rest of Europe for more than a decade. Sastre himself had begun to study Brecht's theoretical writings in 1960, and while he did not accept Brecht's ideas in their totality, he was profoundly influenced by his contact with them. The impact of Brecht on Sastre's dialectical formation likewise leads him to reject his original insistence on the Aristotelian drama's continuing historical validity: ". . . I see that a modern *Poetics* for the theater must take the form of a negation of Brecht's negation of the Aristotelian drama, and can never be a reaffirmation of Aristotelianism in the face of Brechtian criticism"(*AR,* 8). In this respect *Anatomy of Realism* does indeed represent the negation of a basic principle of *Drama and Society.*

Other, less specific aspects of *Drama and Society* are likewise nullified in *Anatomy of Realism*. In general, Sastre notes the youthful naïveté and confusion which had characterized his thought during the composition of *Drama and Society*. The Sastre of 1963 sees the Sastre of the early 1950's as "a sort of socially-oriented nihilist. My 'world view' still consisted basically of nihilism, despair. At best I perceived concrete existence as lacking in sufficient meaning, and sometimes lacking in meaning altogether. I did not even find it possible to find a clear sense in history. I saw socialism as a purely moral imperative and revolution as the only possible meaning for that which surely did not even have a meaning. Although I did feel a need to struggle, *as though it did have a meaning* . . ." (*AR*, 7). In *Drama and Society* Sastre had repeatedly rejected a "political theater" and he had expressed reluctance to accept any significant degree of ideological intrusion by the author; both these attitudes had been based on a fear that the drama would degenerate into propaganda. In *Anatomy of Realism*, he recognizes the naïveté of his earlier position (*AR*, 8).

Despite Sastre's own interpretation of his evolution, however, one must not regard the negation of *Drama and Society* as absolute. Sartre uses *Anatomy of Realism* to reveal and condemn some of his early interpretations and evaluations, but he also uses it to extend some of *Drama and Society*'s major themes: the validity of tragedy, the demand for social responsibility in the writer, the dramatic weakness of unilateral theater, the presence of social injustice in the world and the need to reflect it on the stage, the uselessness of aestheticism, and the ideal literary synthesis of the human condition. The same basic assumption underlies both books: realism is the only valid mode for contemporary literature. And the dissident ethic implied in *Drama and Society* was certainly an embryonic form of the later and more systematic dialectics. Thus, the ideological difference between *Drama and Society* and *Anatomy of Realism* lies not so much in their themes as in the increased sophistication and enlarged factual frame of reference upon which Sastre is able to draw for his second book. The formal difference between them is the presence in *Anatomy of Realism* of a dialectical method of argumentation; the search for synthesis via the rational confrontation of opposites. In this sense the passage from *Drama and Society* to *Anatomy of Realism* is not characterized by a radical reversal, but by intellectual evolution.

In addition to the relation between *Anatomy of Realism* and Sastre's intellectual past, the dialectical vision is also evident in Sastre's explanation of his book's structure. Admitting the weakness of some of the book's earlier essays, Sastre explains that he has nevertheless preferred to include them so that his reader can witness "the surprises and curves in the road" which a writer encounters "as he practices his art" (*AR*, 15). Sastre has conceived his book as something of an intellectual autobiography, and he wants his reader to see the early essays, even though many of them have admittedly been superseded by subsequent changes in their author's attitudes. In other words, Sastre considers it important that his book reflect not only certain ideas, but also the process through which they have been derived. The book's material is generally organized in a chronological way; thus, the reader can indeed visualize the process of affirmation and negation so characteristic of Sastre's intellectual probing. Such a process is perhaps essential to all systematic investigation, but Sastre is sharply aware of its presence in his intellectual life and he consciously cultivates it on different levels as a method of persuasion.

Much of *Anatomy of Realism*'s dialectical conception is thus apparent even without regard to the particular ideological suggestions of its essays. In the text itself the dialectic appears in many forms. Major influences during this period of Sastre's thought are Brecht, Engels, and Georg Lukács; thus, it is not surprising that a Marxist vision of history and society should appear as a correlative to Sastre's dialectical aesthetic theories. To a previously published essay on Brecht, Sastre now appends a new phrase which exalts Brecht as "a man who investigates the true structures of human relations through a profound and subtle understanding of the class struggle . . ." (*AR*, 47-48). Indeed, Sastre's dialectical search for a definition of realism is founded on the assumption that contemporary society is divided into social classes—principally a proletariat and a bourgeoisie—and that the dynamics of human relations are inevitably reflections of class struggle. In support of his contention that literature should be revelation rather than dogma or solution, Sastre quotes Engels' description of realism: "The realism of which I speak . . . has nothing to do with the author's opinions" (*AR*, 30). Sastre defines social literature as "a literature that regards man . . . as a dialectical *relationship* with his environment and with other men" (*AR*, 89, n. 3). Avant-garde literature, which Sastre rejects, is regarded as a symptom of the crisis of a decadent bourgeoisie. *Anatomy of Realism* clearly marks the crystallization of Sastre's Marxist aesthetics.

One can, to be sure, continue also to speak validly of Sastre's existentialism: of his awareness of the asocial aspect of human life, his sympathy for the human being as an isolated, concrete individual on the edge of history and subject to the eternal conditions of being alive and human. Sastre's attempt to reconcile a form of constructive socialism with existentialism is not new in *Anatomy of Realism*, but its conception and articulation are more precise than in his earlier period. The search for a point of equilibrium betwen man's *praxis* and his anguish, his collectivity and his individuality, is, Sastre maintains, the project that gives modern philosophy its form; thus, a relevant contemporary literature must also be conceived in the terms of this task. Both perspectives of man are valid, and Sastre continues to insist that neither must be favored to the exclusion of the other:

> In our attempts to avoid radical nihilism, why should we deny authentic nihility? The rejection of nihilism cannot do away with an awareness of objective nothingness, verifiable at the individual level—the level of the being-for-death. But on the other hand, can we allow that being-for-death to become the sole constant and explanation of human development—i.e., of history? Why reduce all activity, including agony, to *praxis*? How could one fail to postulate a fundamental dialectical relation between the *praxis* and the agony of human activity? Or between the socialization and the interiorization of human reality? How can one resign oneself to anarchistic solitude? To the dissipation of structure? What is the proper extent of individuality? Of socialization? (*AR*, 126-27)

Here Sastre has again formulated the dualistic philosophical framework within which, he maintains, a valid contemporary realism must be developed. He continues to regard realism, in its ideal form, as a dialectical exposition of the conditions of human activity. Tragedy, which is characterized by a superior degree of realism, must also emerge from this dual perspective, and its ideal effect is that of arousing in the spectator an awareness of these same pressures as they apply to his own life. In *Anatomy of Realism* Sastre's prescription for tragedy has remained essentially unchanged from its earlier form: it continues to call for a balanced dramatic form and ideology as the complements of the dualistic philosophical posture which Sastre considers the only valid one: "When tragedy succeeds in transcending the schism—i.e., when it becomes truly tragedy—it situates itself in a superior dialectic which we could perhaps call 'hope'—apart from, or above, any pessimism or optimism that would exclude its opposite" (*AR*, 129).

Anatomy of Realism thus reflects Sastre's continuing belief in an aesthetic ideal to which he gives different names at different moments. In *Anatomy of Realism* he calls it *realismo profundo* (profound realism) and defines it as the "literary mode that includes the tragic quality of individual human existence as well as the perspective of historical development—refusing to disintegrate into pessimism on the one hand, or to offer a naïvely optimistic outlook on the other" (*AR*, 129). This concise definition of realism is a consistent extension of Sastre's search for an effective aesthetic embodiment of human reality. It is also an interesting indication of the influence of Georg Lukács on Sastre's thought during the period of *Anatomy of Realism*. One is impressed by the similarity between Sastre's conception and Lukács' own basic principle of realism:

True great realism . . . depicts man and society as complete entities, instead of showing merely one or the other of their aspects. Measured by this criterion, artistic trends determined by either exclusive introspection or exclusive extraversion equally impoverish and distort reality. Thus realism means a three-dimensionality, an all-roundness, that endows with independent life characters and human relationships. It by no means involves a rejection of the emotional and intellectual dynamism which necessarily develops together with the modern world. All it opposes is the destruction of the completeness of the human personality and of the objective typicality of men and situations through an excessive cult of the momentary mood.[31]

The reader who approaches *Anatomy of Realism* expecting a compact, conclusive definition of realism will be disappointed. The formulation of such a definition is neither the intent nor the accomplishment of Sastre's second book. In fact, after reading *Anatomy and Realism* one would continue to define Sastre's realism as simply as we have previously defined it: Realism is that quality which renders a work of art relevant and complete. What Sastre has actually undertaken in this book is not a compact definition of realism but rather an expanded analysis. As suggested in his book's title, he presents an anatomical description of realism and with varied perspectives he evokes different images of it. He approaches the problem of realism from many different directions: its modern forms, which he now views as reactions against Naturalism, rather than as direct descendents of it; its literary opposites; various forms of pseudo-realism, etc.

The tentative definitions derived from these approaches are complementary parts of a total concept of realism. The common element among the approaches and the definitions they suggest is their dialectical core—an essential element of revelatory, agitational literature. The value of *Anatomy of Realism* lies in its piecemeal illumination of a realism whose totality can be visualized only in terms of its components. Sastre's realism emerges as a process rather than as a formulistic literary mode: a process which consists of a clarifying dialectical movement toward an ideal synthesis. Rather than propose themes or modes, Sastre stresses the process and the agitating, illuminating mission of literature. Literature that effectively fulfills this mission is necessarily realistic: its agitation of spectators or readers affords maximum proof that it is grounded in human reality.

CHAPTER 4

The Theater of Alfonso Sastre

I *Theater as Practical Experience*

ONE will inevitably ask whether Alfonso Sastre, in his own plays, follows the dramatic principles discussed above. Perhaps there is no sound reason for always demanding that a dramatist-theorist do in practice what he advocates in theory, but in Sastre's case the relation between these two areas of endeavor is so essential as to merit consideration. Sastre himself has insisted on the close conceptual relation between his critical work and his creative work: "One might say that my plays are, for me, a means of thinking—although, of course, not the only means. Let me put it this way: my philosophy is 'That is the way it turned out.' This process is due largely to my dramatic—dialectical work."[1] Sastre's theory and theater are mutually illuminating. The dialectical vision that lies at the heart of his dramatic theories has also determined the forms and themes of his dramas, inspiring one critic to characterize Sastre's theater as "the dramatic expression of a dialectic at work."[2]

It should be understood, however, that Sastre's plays are not slavish illustration of preconceived notions of what the drama should be. On the contrary, attitudes and principles central to his theoretical thought often appear in his dramas before being formalized into general theory. In this sense Sastre's plays are frequently experiments which provide the practical experience for subsequent theoretical generalizations.

There are, to be sure, some direct parallels between the inspirations for Sastre's theoretical assertions and the nature of the plays he has written. This is especially true in the matter of influences on his dramatic forms and techniques. *Prólogo patético* (*Pathetic Prologue*), 1950, and *En la red* (*In the Net*), 1959, are tight, Aristotelian dramas.[3] *Escuadra hacia la muerte* (*The Condemned Squad*), 1952, *El pan de todos* (*Community*

Bread), 1953, and *Pathetic Prologue* bear a strong imprint of Jean-Paul Sartre's theater, especially *The Dirty Hands* and *No Exit.* Almost every review of *La mordaza* (*The Gag*), 1954, contains an allusion to the strong echo of O'Neill in the tense, repressed family situation.[4] Upon becoming intrigued with Bertolt Brecht, Sastre decided to attempt his own "epic" drama; the result was *Asalto nocturno* (*Nocturnal Assault*), 1959. And one of Sastre's important recent works, *La sangre y la ceniza* (*The Blood and the Ashes*), 1965, still unpublished and unperformed, is an attempt to find "a certain tragic mode capable of assuming, and somehow surpassing, the experiences of the modern theater."[5] In this play, and in those written after it, Sastre attempts to give dramatic form to principles enunciated in *Anatomy of Realism.*

These developments in Sastre's dramaturgy generally correspond chronologically to the development of his dramatic theories. It is possible, however, to point to attitudes or themes which appear in his essays only after they have appeared in one or more plays. Sastre's sensitivity to the atomic terror that permeates modern life manifests itself in *Uranio 235* (*Uranium 235*), 1946, and *Nocturnal Assault,* long before Sastre expresses that same sensitivity in the introduction to *Las noches lúgubres* (*Lugubrious Nights*), 1963. Modern man's undefined anxiety, also formalized in that essay, is definitely present in *El cuervo* (*The Raven*), 1956. *Cargamento de sueños* (*Cargo of Dreams*), 1946, is an experimental portrayal of the general pain and confusion of being alive and human; in *Drama and Society,* published ten years later, this same existential sensitivity takes its place in Sastre's theory of tragedy. Political revolution is an explicit theme of six of Sastre's plays: *Pathetic Prologue, Community Bread, Tierra roja* (*The Red Earth*), 1954, *Guillermo Tell tiene los ojos tristes* (*Sad Are the Eyes of William Tell*), 1955, *In the Net,* and *Crónicas romanas* (*Roman Chronicles*), 1967. Five of these works were written well before the preface to *Cuatro dramas de la revolución* (*Four Dramas of Revolution*), 1962.

There is thus an obvious interworking between Sastre's theoretical speculation and his dramatic creations. That relation, however, is not simple or linear, but dialectical. It is true that Sastre has often chosen dramatic forms and techniques on the basis of *a priori* assumptions, many of which are reflected in his critical writings. But in matters of ideology, the dramatic formulation has usually preceded the theoretical. Sastre's theater is, as he has often stated, an investigative process. It is an investigation of the conditions of man's existence and activity, and an inquiry into the reasons for his suffering. In the face of his findings Sastre has not been afraid to admit the existence of painful dilemmas and inconsistencies, some of which have posed undeniable contradictions to his original intuitions:

I say that the drama is for me . . . an *investigation* and not an *illustration* of preconceived ideological theses. Now then: this does not mean that I start from an ideological vacuum—no more than do thinkers, researchers, etc. What *is* true is that my "point of departure" may be modified by my dramatic work. This has happened on more than one occasion. In the process of writing a play I have seen my own ideological convictions come in for a harsh examination and subsequent enrichment through a dialectical modification.[6]

The results of Sastre's dramatic investigation have taken their place in the ideologies implicit in his life and his theories. The characteristic dialectic of his theoretical values has thus been present in the very genesis of those theories, in the confrontation between specific experience and theoretical generalization.

There can be no doubt that Sastre does, in his best and most mature plays, adhere to his own theoretical principles. Clearly, his theater is a model of intellectual responsibility, which is the primary exigency of his theories. Other values and concepts central to Sastre's theoretical thought are the investigative function of the drama, a multilateral presentation of the dramatic conflict, and a rounded perspective which makes the characters recognizable both as individual human beings and as members of a social collectivity. His compliance with these principles is, in some plays, only partial or altogether lacking; these cases can validly be considered negative phases of the dialectical process of Sastre's development as dramatist and theorist. It is of the utmost interest and significance that his most effective works for the stage are those in which Sastre's own principles are present and dominant.

II *Theater as Investigation and Revelation*

Sastre regards his theater not only as investigation, but as *criminal* investigation. He begins with the premise that man suffers unjustly, and this injustice implies criminality. Who is the guilty party? This is the fundamental rhetorical question that gives unity to Sastre's varied dramatic production. "I am undertaking an investigation, whose point of departure is the great 'social crimes' and collective suffering of our time. I ask, Who is guilty? And I shall attempt to push on, without vacillation, to the ultimate consequences of this interrogation."[7] Sastre's belief in his investigative mission also provides the conceptual link between his theory and his theater: he visualizes "an investigation with two sides: the theoretical . . . and the strictly *poetic* (the dramatic works). If, on the one hand, I have called for a theater 'founded on the postulates of Realism' and . . . I have defended, with my tenuous strength, the work of the 'testimonial dramatists' (such as Miller and Sartre) and the theses of Upton Sinclair, on the other hand I have always tried to write theater with those same characteristics . . ."[8] Implied in this statement is the principle that the theater can effectively examine (investigate) the human condition only through a revelatory realism. Tragedy, which is characterized by profound realism, is likewise conceived in terms of its investigative function: "I conceive of tragedy as a form of criminal investigation."[9]

We again find ourselves faced with that balanced, dialectical quality which constitutes the very heart of Sastre's approach to theater. "The mission of intellectual and artistic work is to clarify the world," says Sastre, and the world is not clarified if it is presented in the form of imperfect, arbitrary conclusions.[10] Sastre's investigation thus consists of fundamental questions that are never answered conclusively, painful conflicts that are never completely resolved. As José María García Escudero has remarked of Sastre, ". . . his theater is a theater of testimony which he has not wished—or not been able—to turn into a theater of 'solutions.' "[11]

Sastre's theater, in practice as well as in theory, is thus a theater of revelation and agitation, and never a theater of propaganda. "The dramatist's impartiality in the presentation of the case is admirable. Aside from a firm belief in the dignity of man and the worth of human freedom, Sastre betrays no partisanship through his dramas."[12] His awareness that there are multiple ways of viewing every reality is surely one reason for the common view that Sastre's theater is cold, cerebral, bookish, lacking in theatrical force, or that it is theater for minorities.[13] These charges are perhaps true with regard to some of Sastre's plays, and in these cases one would have to entertain the speculation that Sastre's intellectual integrity has, ironically, detracted from his effectiveness as a playwright. But if Sastre's reluctance to admit the existence of moral absolutes has led him to write some bad plays, it has also enabled him to write some very good ones. In his best works for the theater an intellectual richness and dramatic tension derive precisely from Sastre's refusal to pretend that human dilemmas can be resolved painlessly or absolutely.

> Sastre's attitude is a positive one, and represents, on the level of ideas, the courage to be nondogmatic and even undecided in a world where every decision means blindness to a segment of truth—the plight of the modern intellectual. On the level of dramatic craftsmanship, it is a corollary of his belief that dramaturgy is something radically different from propaganda . . .[14]

Given the investigative mission of Sastre's theater, it is only logical that guilt should be one of its recurring themes. Other characteristic themes of his theater are fate, which sometimes seems to be the only explanation for human suffering; human anxiety, fear, and terror (explained or otherwise); war, which is often a concrete source of human anguish; solitude, as a part of the human condition and a source of human suffering; social injustice, as a general or individual affliction, and the corresponding counteractivity in the form of social revolution or personal rebellion; and religious uncertainty.

These themes are predictable correlatives to the ideas and attitudes discussed above. Their persistent presence has led some critics to view Sastre's theater as a pessimistic commentary on modern man.[15] Such an evaluation, however, suggests an incomplete consideration of Sastre's dramatic production. In Sastre's most representative and most effective plays, the frequent suffering and even death which afflict the characters cannot be taken as absolute pronouncements on man's eternal condition. The very fact that Sastre refuses to answer conclusively his own questions suggests not pessimism or optimism, but the *esperanza* (hope) which transcends both these attitudes. Sastre's tragic situations and outcomes are generally left open to the future, open to the possibility that the suffering represented on stage may some day lead to a more just and less painful world. Such a theater cannot be considered pessimistic.

On the other hand, Sastre's expressions of human potentiality are cast entirely in social terms. Consequently, his seven plays which are devoid of social realism would perhaps support an accusation of pessimism. Sastre's theater, like that of Jean-Paul Sartre, is frequently a theater of "situations": a theater in which the protagonist finds himself in a limit situation which demands that he act or be enslaved. When Sastre's characters act to break out of their oppressive situation, they do so in a way that has social implications. When they fail to act and are stifled by their condition, the result is an image of frustration and despair. One will do well to recall Sastre's ideological vacillation in the area of theory, for the presence of seven dramas of frustration in his total production betokens that same mentality in his dramaturgy. In 1963 Sastre used the phrase "a death rattle brought to the stage" with reference to Beckett's theater.[16] He intended the phrase as negative description, but it is applicable to some of his own plays through the year 1956.

Sastre and some critics have preferred to regard these seven plays as ideological accidents; they consider them to be experiments which bear little relation to Sastre's more "representative" dramas of social agitation.[17] It is true that Sastre's importance as a dramatist has not been greatly enhanced by any of these seven plays; they are, for different reasons, less than exciting theater. It is also true that the last of these plays, *The Raven,* was written in 1956. Statistically, furthermore, these works constitute less than one-third of Sastre's total dramatic production and less than twenty percent of his mature, full-length theater. In this sense they are not typical of Sastre's work. But before dismissing these plays as "not representative" one should consider that the most representative thing about Sastre's intellectual life is his struggle to find an alternative to nihilism. A small part of his dramatic production is vivid testimony to the gaping ideological chasm that would result should the struggle be lost.

III *Classifications of Sastre's Plays*

A classification of Sastre's plays according to their image of man would thus consist of two major categories, each analogous to one dimension of Sastre's existentialist-socialist framework. On the one hand would be the seven dramas of frustration: *Ha sonado la muerte* (*Death Has Sounded*), 1946, *Uranium 235*, *Cargo of Deams*, *Comedia sonámbula* (*Sleepwalker's Comedy*), 1947, *Anna Kleiber*, 1955, *La sangre de Dios* (*The Blood of God*), 1955, and *The Raven.* These plays offer a world in which action is impossible and individuals are overcome by their circumstances. This is a theater lacking in social perspective; its characters live in a world of individual anguish, isolated from their social collectivity and from the movement of history. Sastre's dramas of frustration consequently do not comply with their author's theoretical insistence upon a dual, balanced image of man in the drama.

Opposed in their human image to the dramas of frustration are Sastre's dramas of possibility. They include the remainder of his production: *Pathetic Prologue*, *El cubo de la basura* (*The Garbage Pail*), 1951, *The Condemned Squad*, *Community Bread*, *The Gag*, *The Red Earth*, *Sad Are the Eyes of William Tell*, *Muerte en el barrio* (*Death in the Neighborhood*), 1965, *In the Net*, *Nocturnal Assault*, *La cornada* (*Death Thrust*), 1959, *Oficio de tinieblas* (*Office of Darkness*), 1962, *The Blood and the Ashes*, *La taberna fantástica* (*The Fantastic Tavern*), 1966, *El banquete* (*The Banquet*), 1967, and *Roman Chronicles*, 1968. Although varied in form and focus, these plays have in common a basic philosophical suggestion: action is possible, and man must act in order to give meaning to his life. Thus, the characters of these plays, unlike those of the dramas of frustration, are not completely stifled by their existence. They succeed in acting upon their circumstances and, through their own initiative, they alter the situation of which they are a part. Even though their actions usually produce painful and ambiguous results, the characters of these plays at least live in a world where man can *hope* to better his lot. The world of these dramas of possibility is a world in which the forces of oppression are not entirely beyond the understanding of those who suffer, for in these dramas the agents of suffering and indignity are largely social in nature. The acts which the characters commit in their attempts to recover their personal dignity thus have social significance. The potential for action which characterizes Sastre's dramas of possibility is due directly to his social perspective of man, present in these plays but absent from the dramas of frustration.

A general classification of Sastre's theater according to its forms and techniques produces a division similar to a division on the basis of the plays' human image. The dramas of frustration are essentially experimental in form. Such disconcerting elements as narration, dreams, flashbacks, and radical distortions of time and space are used to give dramatic form to the senseless world implicit in these dramas.

The dramas of possibility fall into two groups. The first includes the plays in which Sastre has cultivated the "penetrative realism" so insistently advocated in his theories of the drama: a realism which avoids superficial naturalistic imitation, observes basic Aristotelian principles of unity, and attempts to uncover the existential and social tensions of modern man. This group of plays constitutes the bulk of Sastre's production and includes *Pathetic Prologue, The Garbage Pail, The Condemned Squad, Community Bread, The Gag, The Red Earth, Sad Are the Eyes of William Tell, Death in the Neighborhood, In the Net, Death Thrust,* and *Office of Darknes.*

The second group of dramas of possibility, and the third major direction of Sastre's theater, is his most recent tendency, which might be termed "post-Brechtian." Since 1965 Sastre has avoided Artistotelian dramatic principles and has concentrated instead on a theater based on the principles of alienation and distantiation, generally associated with Bertolt Brecht. Sastre's post-Brechtian plays are *The Blood and the Ashes, The Fantastic Tavern, The Banquet,* and *Roman Chronicles.* An antecedent to these plays is *Nocturnal Assault,* in which Sartre employs some Brechtian techniques but does not exploit them as fully as he does in his later plays of the same tendency.

These brief classifications suggest a clear relation between the worlds reflected in Sastre's plays and the techniques used to bring those worlds to life on the stage. Sastre has stated that his dramatic forms always correspond to the material presented in a given play.[18] As we shall see below, this assertion is generally true, although use of the adverb "always" constitutes an overstatement. A study of Sastre's twenty-three works for the theater on the basis of the foregoing classifications will further clarify this relation between form and content.

CHAPTER 5

The Dramas of Frustration

I *The Arte Nuevo Plays*

SASTRE'S first four plays are also his first four dramas of frustration. These experimental one-act works represent Sastre's contributions to the effort of Arte Nuevo, the youthful theater group with which he worked from 1946 to 1948.[1] The forms and themes of these plays offer a vivid representation of the nihilistic despair so characteristic of Sastre's early years.

The least impressive of the four is *Sleepwalker's Comedy.* It employs the same avant-garde techniques as the other plays of this period, but uses them to little advantage. *Sleepwalker's Comedy* is a poorly conceived, vaguely symbolic treatment of the eternal dreams and wanderings which are the stuff of human existence. Cyrus C. DeCoster calls it "a surrealistic fantasy in which the dramatist makes use of dreams to emphasize the chaotic incoherence of life. But it is a confused work; its symbolism is murky and it lacks focus."[2]

In *Death Has Sounded* and *Uranium* 235 the terror of war hovers in the background as the source of the agony in which the characters writhe. In spite of this theme, however. these plays are hardly comparable to Sastre's dramas of social agitation. In his first two works Sastre does not treat war as humanity's greatest madness or as a manifestation of social injustice. The fact that war is made by men becomes almost incidental as Sastre elevates its terror to a metaphysical, anonymous level. The subject of the two plays is agony and death, and Sastre's implication is that these phenomena come from uncontrollable sources which are not concretely human. *Death Has Sounded*, which bears the subtitle "Stage Account in One Act," is openly inspired by Thornton Wilder's novel, *The Bridge of San Luis Rey*; it attempts to discover the reason why one member of a household happened to leave the house only moments before it and its occupants were destroyed by bombs. Wilder was also the inspiration for the play's narrative form and anticlimactic structure.[3] The narrator, a European correspondent for the New York *Herald*, says in his opening speech to the audience: "And then I thought about Thornton Wilder and about that marvelous account of life and death, *The Bridge of San Luis Rey*. And I could not get away from that question Wilder always has on his mind: 'Why?' That 'Why' that is always there—in the eyes of a child . . . in the smile of an old man. Why did my friend Bernard survive? Why were the others killed?"[4]

The entire play is an attempt to answer this question through an examination of Bernard's life and a scrutiny of the circumstances of the catastrophe. In his final summary the narrator tentatively suggests several explanations, but none is satisfactory: "I realize that we have hardly resolved anything, and that that anguished 'Why?' is still floating in the air."[5] The play is thus an investigation on several levels, and the theme of fate emerges as fundamental. In addition to the specific investigation which constitutes its plot, *Death Has Sounded* points toward an equally futile attempt to rationalize all the senseless catastrophies of human life: "Isn't living merely an attempt to understand life?"[6] The sense of fatalistic inevitability is enhanced by the early revelation of the climax, the flashback technique, and the presence on stage of a clock which moves relentlessly toward the hour at which the bombs will fall.

The point of departure for *Uranium 235* was Sastre's horrified reaction to the atomic bombardment of Hiroshima and Nagasaki only months before he wrote this play. *Uranium 235* begins with a speech in which Professor Rufus, a character from H.G. Wells's *The World Set Free*, enthusiastically informs the audience of the great advances which the development of atomic energy will bring to humanity. His predictions prove to be ironic. He is interrupted, the prologue ends, and the scene becomes a desolate mountain sanitarium where a sick humanity comments on the atomic holocaust which has just destroyed two Japanese cities. Gradually these patients die, except for Mara and her sweetheart, Benjamín, who leave the sanitarium and go back out into the world. They will be the Adam and Eve of a new humanity. There are suggestions of symbolism in the sanitarium (a sick world), its inhabitants (a humanity whose survival is tentative), Mara and Benjamín (biblical characters who are the hope for humanity's regeneration), and their son, Iván (humanity's fresh start and new hope). Iván suddenly becomes a young man of twenty years and the play ends with a dual possibility for the future: either man will turn to God, or he will destroy himself. Sastre chooses to end the play with an affirmation of God's goodness and, implicitly, of humanity's future: "I have seen God. He is not dead. He loves us more than ever. He is beautiful, he is with men of good will. He will save us."[7] In the play's final speech Iván finds reassurance in the Bible: "'And the earth was without form, and void; and darkness was upon the face of the deep. And the spirit of God moved upon the face of the waters . . .'"(*OC*, 30).

But as so frequently happens, Sastre's attempt at optimism appears to be forced and in conflict with his immediate inclinations. The play's ending is arbitrary: a pessimistic ending would have been perfectly consistent with the rest of the work. Furthermore, Iván discovers the Bible only moments after he has found another book with entirely different implications for the future: *Uranium 235*. Thus, the spectator, and probably Sastre, is not convinced that faith in God will be sufficient to keep man from destroying the world and himself.

Cargo of Dreams is the best of Sastre's early plays. It represents a mentality which Sastre himself would later criticize and a form of theater which he would generally avoid, but it is one of the few powerful and important pieces written for the Spanish stage during the 1940's. Like the other works Sastre wrote for Arte Nuevo, *Cargo of Dreams* is vague and symbolic. Its characters are victims of their existence rather than dominators of it. José María de Quinto considers this play to be "the first breakthrough of an existentialist vision in the postwar Spanish theater."[8] Ricardo Domenech calls it a "pre-Beckett play."[9]

Domenech applies to *Cargo of Dreams* a criticism that Sastre has frequently invoked against Beckett's theater: it presents man as "an abstract entity, a 'wanderer' who, from the depths of solitude and incomprehension, tries to come to grips with the great mystery of his existence." This play fails, says Domenech, to consider man as a part of history and it refuses to invoke history's rational constants which might clarify somewhat the human condition. Its image of man is therefore incomplete.[10] Whether or not this quality is a defect depends on one's critical criteria, but there is no doubt that in *Cargo of Dreams* human agony prevails over human potentiality. Man is presented as a helpless, useless creature in an absurd universe: "This play offers us a man, or rather Man: alone, abandoned, living in an unreal world that he does not understand, overwhelmed by time and caught in the web of his own makeup. Man . . . who kills that which he loves and wanders aimlessly until death comes for him. Fragility of the human being, solitude, incomprehension, the absurdity of life."[11]

In *Cargo of Dreams* Sastre again uses the narrative flashback technique. The principal character, Man, tells the story of his life to an enigmatic interlocutor, Jeschoua. As he evokes the characters of his past, they appear on stage. Man tells Jeschoua: "Something keeps getting between me and truth. A dear, absurd obstacle. A stupid crutch. Dreams. What if I turned out to be a dream? A useless passion, an error in space? The things around me don't even know I'm here. I don't exist for them. They don't exist either. No one sees them. Sphinxes. Yes! Sphinxes . . . horribly peaceful in their death, while I am simply something behind a mask . . . a biological mistake" (*OC*, 41). The only solidarity Man has found, the only weight he bears, is the labyrinth of vague dreams which constitute his reality and his torment: "Do you know what I drag along with me? A cargo of dreams. Like all humanity. It's like a caravan which for centuries has been dragging its terrible cargo of dreams. It's all so vague, so unreal . . ." (*OC*, 152-53). His intuition tells him there must be some meaning in human existence: "Yes, there must be a reason . . . an enormous reason. Because some awful things are happening here" (*OC*, 154). His love affair with Frau appears to provide that meaning for his life, but it proves to be illusion. Crazed by the knowledge of her infidelity, Man kills the only person he had loved. The play's final scene is a symbolic chess game between Man and Death. Death wins easily.

II *Later Dramas of Frustration*

One critic has written that the four plays written for Arte Nuevo are irrelevant to any consideration of Sastre's evolution as a dramatist, "since their own author regards them as the uncertain groping of a period in which his dramatic position was still undefined."[12] The logic of this position is highly dubious, most obviously because the study of evolution implies comparison, and comparison cannot be carried out if one excludes annoying anomalies. And regardless of this logical consideration, the four plays Sastre wrote for Arte Nuevo are, in their form and ideology, definite antecedents to three of his later plays: *The Raven, The Blood of God,* and *Anna Kleiber.*

Around 1950 Sastre becomes aware of the theater's social potential, and most of his subsequent works have a social perspective not to be found in those under consideration; this, of course, is the evolution to which Sr. Aragonés refers. But even though Sastre's socializing tendency grows ever stronger, it does not develop in a linear manner. His characteristic intellectual tension and vacillation produce occasional asocial plays of confusion and despair until the year 1956. These works do not fulfill Sastre's own later requirements for effective theater, but they cannot simply be dismissed. They are the imaginative counterpart to the vacillation of Sastre's theoretical thought, and the mentality that produces *The Raven, The Blood of God,* and *Anna Kleiber* is the mentality that produced the works written for Arte Nuevo.

The full-length play most obviously related to Sastre's earlier period is *Anna Kleiber,* an elaboration of the frustrated relationship between Man and Frau in *Cargo of Dreams.*[13] In *Anna Kleiber* the narrative technique is exploited more fully than in *Cargo of Dreams* and Sastre's alteration of the time sequence is more radical, but the image of a humanity suffocated by its own existence is the same. "We again find the pessimism of the early plays, and the implicit accusation hurled at a God who allows his creatures to writhe in pain, fear, and incomprehension."[14]

The play is essentially a case study of a woman whose sadistic and masochistic compulsions lead her to destroy herself and all who come into contact with her. That the theme is not exactly original, and Sastre's presentation of it a bit tedious, has been persistently pointed out by critics, most of whom consider the play one of Sastre's least successful efforts.[15] *Anna Kleiber* does, indeed, recall theatrical styles and conventions of the recent past: the fashionable neurotics of the twentieth-century stage, the rather self-conscious use of cinematic techniques. One may even see in *Anna Kleiber* a kinship with the Romantic drama, insofar as Sastre's play is a grotesque parody of the standard Romantic situation: separation and frustration of lovers, culminating in a final reunion in death.

The plot of *Anna Kleiber* consists of a long, frustrated love affair between Anna and Alfredo Merton. The source of the repeated separation of the lovers is Anna's perverse character which causes her constantly to undermine the very love and tranquility she seeks. In one of her confessions of infidelity she tells Alfredo: "To keep my love for you, to make it grow, I had to feel dirty, to corrupt myself . . . so that you would appear in my memory like some pure marvel who didn't deserve me, like something adorable . . ."[16] Anna's death provides the ultimate frustration of their love, but paradoxically it also ends the tortured frustration caused by the lovers' futile attempts to find harmony in each other. Alfredo suggests as much in his final words to his dead mistress:

> You're dead, Anna. God didn't want us to find each other again. . . . But now I have you. You're dead, Anna, and now you can't run away. You're here for me. I know that everything must be born again, and then you won't be able to go back to your madness, and I'll have you for my own. Until then, keep her, Death! With you she's at peace. Now I don't need to worry about you. I have you. Now no one but me can kiss Anna Kleiber . . . no one else can put his arms around her waist or feel the touch of her legs . . . (p. 155)

The suggestion of a possible reunion and consolation in death is repeated at the end of the play, as the narrator tells Alfredo: ". . . the two of you may well find each other again—and for always—if it is true that the body will rise again . . ."[17] Any appearance of optimism in this hope for the future, however, is illusory. After such a sordid panorama of misadventures, any attempt at optimism would inevitably be unconvincing. It appears likely that Sastre included these lines as an ironic device: if one's hope for happiness lies in death, the implicit commentary on human life is obvious. There is no doubt that the spectator will be more convinced by Alfredo's "infinite grief" than by the likelihood of its disappearance.

As in two of his earlier plays, Sastre situates the action of *Anna Kleiber* against the background of World War Two. Again, however, it would be difficult to find overtones of social injustice in this background action. It certainly reveals Sastre's constant preoccupation with war and it serves as a device for characterization and plot development, but Anna is neither the victim nor the product of the war around her. She is, rather, the victim of herself and of the dark forces that make suffering inevitable in human life. "Sastre's real subject . . . is the inadequacy of love for human fulfillment; it is this dark, deep force in men . . . which eternally rejects happiness."[18] What is this force? Why is it an inevitable part of human existence? These are the questions Sastre leaves unanswered in *Anna Kleiber*.

The same unanswered questions are posed in a different form in *The Raven*, usually regarded as the most complete anomaly of Sastre's seven asocial dramas. Unlike the other dramas of frustration, *The Raven* employs a traditional form. It is a tight, unified drama in two acts. It has no narrator, and its characterization and setting are naturalistic. The experimental feature of this play is not its structure, but rather the disturbing events that occur within a traditional dramatic framework.

The Raven consists of a series of unnatural or supernatural occurrences which are never fully explained. The characters thus find themselves in a situation which, unlike the dramatic situations of some of Sastre's works, does not offer an escape to one willing to exercise his liberty. The characters of *The Raven* are not free to act or to break dramatically from their situation. They are helpless; they can only watch and suffer as invisible monsters play diabolical games with their hopes for happiness.

Four friends—Juan, Alfonso, Pedro, and Inés—are gathered in Juan's isolated home on New Year's Eve. Gradually they realize they are reliving events which took place precisely a year ago. This discovery horrifies them, for on New Year's Eve of the previous year Juan's wife, Laura, was brutally murdered by a lunatic in the garden. Now the friends discover that every detail of their present situation, including their very presence in Juan's house, matches their situation at the same time a year ago. Somehow they have been brought together to relive the events of that horrible night. As the characters become aware of the supernatural thing that is happening to them, their thoughts turn to Laura and they wonder if she will join them, as she did one year before.

At the end of the first act Laura comes down the stairs. She has been upstairs resting and remembers having experienced nothing unusual. Through a strange relativity of time, Laura has not yet experienced the events of her death, while her companions are now living that fatal evening for the second time. They try desperately to devise a plan to prevent the repetition of Laura's murder. The previous year, when Laura went into the garden and was killed, no one was able to help her because the friends' merriment and intoxicated condition had kept them from hearing her screams. Thus they resolve to maintain a sober vigil, hoping that the fatal hour will pass—this time without tragedy. But their precautions prove futile. All except Laura are suddenly seized by a spell that paralyzes them and deadens their senses. A knock is heard at the door; Laura, at first terrified, suddenly walks naturally to the door, opens it, and goes out to her death. The others recover their senses in time to hear her screams but too late to save her. They run out into the snow but find no trace of her. Juan realizes that she has gone forever, and he and Alfonso underline this fact by quoting extensively from Edgar Allan Poe's "The Raven."

One critic has aptly described *The Raven* as "a mystery play with metaphysical connotations."[19] This critic correctly insists on the theme of relativity and reversibility of time in this play.[20] It should be noted, however, that the play's transcendence is not limited to this theme. As the catastrophe approaches, the mystery element diminishes and the metaphysical connotations grow stronger. The attempts of the characters to define and guard against the force that threatens them leads to the clear image of an anonymous evil which lurks in the shadows, waiting to prevent or destroy man's happiness. The enemy is terrifying, precisely because of his vagueness: "Who is there? If he is an enemy, why don't we hear his voice, his threats? Why can't we at least know what we're up against? If he is a friend, why doesn't he offer us an occasional kind word? Anything except leaving us like this . . . alone and afraid in this old house. Like wretched children on a winter night. Why?" (*OC*, 706). Men have given the name "God' to the force that controls human destiny. Is God, then, to be defined as a monster who reaches from the shadows to snatch away the happiness that he dangles before his victims?[21] "A single eye that stares at us from the shadows. . . . Someone or something is there. He doesn't change. It terrifies us to think about him. . . . We don't understand him. What does he want from us? Could it be . . . God?" (*OC*, 706). Is human life finite, or does it somehow transcend this suffering that afflicts all men? "It may be that we are more than merely this time that passes: Who knows?" (*OC*, 712). Again, pain, confusion, and death lead to the eternal questions of man's existence. And again Sastre does not answer these questions. *The Raven* is Sastre's "almost delirious form of protest, like a scream in the night" against an evil that has yet to be defined.[22]

The existence and nature of God are again questioned, this time explicitly, in *The Blood of God,* which Sastre calls an "homage to Kierkegaard." Luis Opuls calls unexpectedly at the gloomy old home of his former professor, Jacobo Parthon. In Luis's early dialogue with Pathon's son, Ben, and with Parthon himself, the theme of faith is exposed and developed. Luis cites Abraham as history's greatest example of blind faith: Abraham, who was prepared to follow God's orders even to the point of killing his own son. Luis's telling of this story and Ben's horrified reaction to it prepare the spectator for the drama's critical moment at the end of Act One. At this point Professor Parthon will become a latter-day Abraham; he will be faced with the choice of either proving his faith by killing his son, or failing to obey what he believes to be God's instructions.

A discussion of God's nature emerges from the discussion of faith. Sastre develops two opposing images of God through the opposite views of Parthon and Luis. According to Parthon, God suffers with the suffering of his creatures: "I believe that with every drop of blood spilt in this world, God's blood is shed, too. . . . God is the first one who suffers when men suffer . . ." (*OC*, 492). Luis, on the other hand, sees God as something quite different: "God seems like something different . . . something absolutely alien. Strange . . . unknown . . . immobile . . . cold . . . unchanging. . . . You know what I mean? Something fixed—something not even capable of shuddering. Something serene and quiet, invisible, unconcerned about this flood of human suffering—this river of slime and blood where you see dead bodies of children and hear the screams of alcoholics. . . . Impassive, unconcerned, and unknown. That's God isn't it?" (*OC*, 492-93). Luis's view is supported by Parthon's wife, whose agony at the recent death of her elder son caused her to scream, "Either God does not exist, or He is a monster" (*OC*, 492). Thus Sastre makes explicit in *The Blood of God* an idea at which he hints in several other plays.

The duality established in the play's early moments is never resolved. Sastre continues the implicit debate over God's nature right to the end of the play by means of an artificial but interesting double denouement. First, Parthon kills his son, having heard—or thought he heard—God tell him to do so. His trial, which takes place in the following scene, has the tone of a criminal investigation: the two attorneys debate Parthon's crime in an attempt to explain the presence of such an absurdity in the world. Implicitly they discuss and try to raltionalize all gratuitous acts that cause men to suffer. Their failure to find an explanation is reflected in the plea of the defense: Parthon is insane; his act (or God's) cannot be explained by "normal psychology." Parthon is sent to a mental institution. His faith remains firm, even after he returns home and finds himself hated by his wife. God has left him alone, but as the episode ends Parthon shouts desperately and repeatedly: "I believe in God!" (*OC*, 522).

The play's final scene is the alternate fate Parthon might have had if God had not abandoned him in his moment of need. The action goes back to the moment just before Parthon is to kill Ben. This time the episode transpires as in the biblical story of Abraham. Just as the knife is about to fall, a scream is heard from the garden. Sofía, Ben's sweetheart, has been strangely compelled to come to the Parthon home; while crossing the garden she has been attacked by the family's usually harmless old dog. Parthon rushes into the garden and kills the dog, rather than his son. Thus, in the play's alternate denouement a God of love, satisfied with his creature's demonstration of faith, intercedes, as in the Old Testament, by providing an angel and a sacrificial lamb.

The play's ideological and structural center is Professor Parthon's faith, which is constant in both versions of the conclusion. "Parthon, offering up his son in holocaust, is the 'hero' of faith —a faith carried out in total anguish and in blind obedience to an absurd God capable of a gratuitous crime."[23] The meaning of his faith, however, varies radically from one denouement to the other. The first portrayal is of a capricious, uncaring God who induces men to commit acts which become absurd when their consequences are meaningless or painfully ironic. In this case, or in the event that God does not exist, religious faith is reduced to self-delusion, hallucination, or insanity. Its rewards are loneliness and death. If, on the other hand, God is the God of love and mercy, the God of Abraham, then faith is rewarded by life rather than by death. In this case, faith and life give meaning to each other. The first possibility is the view of Luis Opuls, the second that of Professor Parthon. Both are presented as having equal possible validity. Sastre refuses to answer his own theological question, either within the play or in his commentaries on it: "I prefer not to give an opinion on the theological problem, which might be formulated as follows: Is it conceivable that the God of the New Testament could order such a sacrifice?" (*OC*, 479). The author's own impartiality is supported by the very form of his play, in the use of an experimental double denouement.

CHAPTER 6

The Dramas of Social Realism

I *Minor Social Dramas*

SASTRE'S twelve dramas of social realism are also theater of investigation, revelation, and agitation. They are based on the pressures which certain situations or a general human condition bring to bear on human beings, and they offer no conclusive answers or solutions. Unlike the works discussed above, however, Sastre's dramas of social realism comply with their author's principle that the drama should present characters who are not only creatures of anguish but also men of action: human beings in their historical, social function as well as their timeless existential predicament. Sastre has made an obvious commitment to the cause of human freedom, but the dramatic quality of his best theater is due precisely to his realization that freedom is a dialectical, rather than a unilateral, reality. Man's struggle for social liberty must always be tempered by a concern for his individual integrity; otherwise, revolutionary activity would only succeed in exchanging one form of oppression for another. In Sastre's theater the struggle for freedom is never simple. Sastre does not indulge in facile heroism or vilification. An oppressed individual or group may triumph, but the success is never easy or naïve. Sastre's characters are never supermen. With regard to both his theories and his dramatic works, Sastre can speak honestly of an "excruciating tension between ethics and politics, between the needs of the inner life and those of the socializing process, between concrete existence and history."[1]

In their settings as well as their action, these dramas reflect their author's search for social realism. In contrast to the vague, often irrelevant settings of the dramas of frustration, Sastre's social dramas take place in a world that inevitably imposes an awareness of social injustice and responsibility. The action's geographical location is not always apparent, but its social significance is unmistakable. A country that lives in tyranny, a working-class neighborhood, the lives of revolutionary activists, or human relations based on exploitation provide an eminently social background to the action of a given drama. The dimensions of the dramatic situation constitute the limits within which a character is required to commit a painful act of social and personal consequence.

Of course, the incorporation of ideological ambiguity and a dual perspective of man do not guarantee good theater, and some of Sastre's works are dramatically unsuccessful in spite of the presence of these elements. These dramas are ineffective for "technical" reasons, but more fundamentally it seems that they are deficient because Sastre has complied with his dramatic principles only partially or unevenly. *The Garbage Pail,* for example, attempts to portray the circumstances of revolutionary activity. But the play is fragmented because the collective movement provides only a vague background to the actions of the protagonist, Germán. Germán does not even believe in the validity of this movement. "You know, I don't believe in 'social injustice,' Mr. Tom. The only injustices I believe in are the ones people do to me. The police or the union can't help me out. The way I see it, everybody has to make his own justice" (*OC*, 120). Germán acts to give his life meaning outside this movement, by killing a scoundrel who was mistreating a girl. He is motivated by personal emotional factors. Even though by killing this man he presumably removes a bit of social injustice from the world, neither he nor his act is related to the political revolution that brews in the background.

In fairness to Sastre, however, it should be pointed out that *The Garbage Pail* is one of his earliest plays, and that it was written before his dialectical aesthetic principles had matured. Furthermore, the weak relation between the protagonist's life and the drama's collective movement was precisely what Sastre wanted:

> Two orders are involved in *The Garbage Pail*: the personal order and the social order. The man who commits the crime is merely an anarchist, a product of our time. He is indifferent toward collective movements, skeptical about social justice (and, logically enough, about so-called social injustice). He is a man who believes simply that one must make his own justice. The attitude toward the invisible antagonist provokes in this man no social anguish, no sense of class struggle. We see here an example of a perfect anti-Marxist. In this

play the social order goes its own way, functioning independently of the personal tragedy which unfolds before us. Therein is reflected the tragic inequality of the classes and the dialectic of the struggle. (*OC*, 109)

Sastre's explanation of this early play thus reveals a clear perception of the Marxist principles that were to characterize his future work, but the play itself suggests an immature sense of their effective dramatic translation.

The same general criticism can be made of *Office of Darkness*. In a very obvious manner this play suggests a criminal investigation, for it is essentially a mystery play. Miguel, the protagonist, thinks he is guilty of having killed a girl during a drunken spree the previous night. He does not remember the night's events, but his companions, who were with him during the spree and are with him now in a country chalet, have informed him of his guilt. Gradually Miguel and the audience become aware that the guilty party is not Miguel, but rather one of his companions. *Office of Darkness*, like *The Garbage Pail*, suffers from a weak relation between the plot and its broader social implications. The false friends who have framed Miguel are *pieds noirs* who have taken refuge in Spain. This fact provides opportunity for commentary on the evils of fanatical colonialism, but Sastre fails to exploit the possibilities. The characters' affiliation with the *pieds noirs* is irrelevant to the plot, and Miguel's situation remains a purely personal dilemma which costs him his life.

The major defect of *Community Bread* and *Sad Are the Eyes of William Tell* is a slightly different one. In these plays the problem is not so much a lack of relation between the social and individual crises as it is Sastre's failure to develop sufficiently one or the other. In some respects *Community Bread* is typical of Sastre's dramas of revolution. The action takes place in a Communist country that is still in its revolutionary phase, and the revolution's social and political changes are not easily achieved. With admirable integrity Sastre insists on the relativity of social values; he shows that the revolutionary ideal is inevitably subject to contamination by individual egos and that a political system can be established and defended only through a pragmatic distortion of truth. David Harko, the protagonist, is a young Party official who refuses to recognize the inherent relativity of the revolution's ideals. His absolute fidelity to the Cause leads him to denounce the Party Commissar, who is guilty of profiteering. David acts in full awareness that he is sending his mother to the gallows, for she too is a profiteer and will be implicated by the Commissar.[2] The play's ideological ambiguity, embodied in David's torment and in the suicide to which it ultimately drives him, proved to be sufficiently effective, when the play was staged in Barcelona in 1957, to provoke alternate attacks from both ends of the political spectrum (*OC,* 225-26).

But even though *Community Bread* is a good portrayal of an individual in a limit situation, and a sensitive exposition of ideological ambiguities, one cannot avoid the feeling that David's act is somewhat abritrary, perhaps monstrous. Most of what the spectator knows about the revolution is transmitted to him indirectly, through dialogue. He sees very little immediate evidence of the problems which beset the country's effort to establish a just social order. On the other hand, he is saturated with David's own absolutism, his individual decision, and his subsequent torment. There is thus a disproportionate emphasis on the individual and a deficient exposition of the social context. Consequently, David's decision to let his mother die is not very convincing, because the spectator is not sufficiently familiar with the factors that lead to that decision. Sastre would later state explicitly that a strong inclusion of a character's social context can be an effective means of avoiding melodrama.[3] Had he been aware of this fact when he wrote *Community Bread,* perhaps he would have avoided some of the melodrama and sentimentality that detract so seriously from that play's effectiveness.

In *Sad Are the Eyes of William Tell* it is the individual character, rather than the social context, that is insufficiently developed. The spectator of this drama witnesses many examples of the ruthless tyranny from which Tell finally liberates his country. An old blind man is machine-gunned on stage, the town's citizens are forced to bow before the tyrant's hat placed on a pike in the town square, police are shown as brutal imbeciles, the Governor's attendants are half-witted lackeys, and the Governor himself is a sadistic drunkard. The need for revolution is clear, but the man who precipitates the revolt is almost a stranger to the audience. The play's last two scenes are quite moving in their depiction of this modern William Tell who suddenly finds himself caught in a limit situation, is forced to act alone, and finally to accept the consequences of his act: loneliness, pain, and confusion. But it is doubtful that Tell's exposure prior to the play's climactic scene has been sufficient to arouse the audience's empathy. Sastre's drama of the William Tell whose arrow goes astray and kills his son is in many ways one of his cleverest and most sensitive works, and the play's defects are partially compensated by its positive attributes. But Sastre obviously intended this play not only as a grotesque parody of dictatorships, but also as the drama of an Existentialist man whose act creates meaningful repercussions at the expense of personal tranquillity. The work's total effectiveness is unfortunately limited by the imperfection of that difficult balance which Sastre himself prescribes.

In spite of its dramatic weakness, however, *Sad Are the Eyes of William Tell* is clearly the most captivating and most important of the plays which we have termed "minor social dramas." Sastre's reworking of the William Tell legend gives it a powerful contemporary relevance and allows the consummation of the tragedy which, according to Sastre, is implicit in the story of William Tell but has always been aborted by other writers who have dealt with the matter (*OC*, 587-88). Sastre's protagonist, unlike the triumphant hero of earlier versions of the legend, is a demythified human being who doubts, suffers, and commits a hideous error that makes the success of the revolution bitterly ironic. He is a man who never wanted to "get involved" in the revolutionary cause, a man who has no heroic aspirations. He ultimately assumes leadership of the revolution, not out of a sense of duty or desire for power, but simply as a furious reaction against the Governor who had caused his son's death.

In *Sad Are the Eyes of William Tell* certain theatrical devices appear for the first time in Sastre's theater. The long ballad in Scene i, with which the old blind man sings the atrocities of the Governor, is a bit of agile versification and represents Sastre's new interest in the use of musical narrative in the drama. Black humor appears for the first time in Sastre's theater. Especially notable in this respect is the play's brilliant climax—Scene vi—surely one of the finest scenes in all of Sastre's work. Here Sastre uses black humor and caricature in a withering attack on dictatorships and servile citizens who tolerate them:

GOVERNOR. Wait a minute. (*Silence. The* GOVERNOR *wobbles.*) I feel a bit ill. I shall now vomit. Then we'll deal with that other matter.

GUARD 1. Vomit? Right here. On me. Please, sir, it will be an honor. Vomit on me, sir. I'll never forget it. Thank you, sir.

GOVERNOR. (*Heaves.*) Christ . . . I'm sick.

GUARD 1. On me, sir! On me! (*Writhes on the ground.*)

GOVERNOR. (*Panting.*) There. That's better. (*OC*, 644)

The clichés that dictatorships employ as a rationale are subjected to biting parody:

AID 1. (*Interrupting enthusiastically.*) There is no reason to be sad! None whatsoever! We can look confidently to the future! All is going well! Extremely well! Highways are being built! The living standard of the working class is rising! We have freedom of the press—except for lies and errors. Prior to the administration of Admiral General Gessler, this country was choked by chaos, corruption, barbarism! Gessler has brought peace, progress, law and order, joy! The proletariat is happy! Everyone is so happy! (*He bursts into tears and crumples to the ground like a rag, sobbing convulsively. Two guards grab him and drag him off. The* GOVERNOR *looks on understandingly and comments:*)

GOVERNOR. Poor thing. He's tired. He's been working rather hard. (*OC*, 645)

Sad Are the Eyes of William Tell occupies an important place in Sastre's artistic development and it features some of his most brilliant writing. One suspects that a skillful production could largely compensate for the play's uneven dramatic quality.

II *Dramas of Personal Rebellion*

The remaining examples of Sastre's social realism more successfully achieve a fusion of the metaphysical and the earthly, the individual and the collective, the existential and the social. As a result of this balance, the dramatic power of these plays is greater than is that of the works discussed above. In *The Condemned Squad, The Gag, Death in the Neighborhood,* and *Death Thrust,* Sastre chooses to treat the problem of individual rebellion, or self-assertion in the context of a difficult situation, as compared to other social dramas which deal directly with some aspect of social or political revolution. The difference between the two themes is of course one of perspective, in that all these dramas present the individual in terms of his relation to social or political structures.

The Condemned Squad is a splendidly balanced allegory of the human condition, heavy with transcendental overtones which reverberate at many levels. The members of the condemned squad are stationed in a lonely cabin. World War Three is in progress, and the men tensely await the start of an expected enemy offensive. Their mission is suicidal: it is assumed that the awaited encounter with the enemy will be fatal. They have been sent on this mission as punishment for various crimes which are revealed gradually. The squad is commanded by Corporal Goban, a fanatical disciplinarian who forces his men to live in the strictest military propriety, even though in their situation nothing could be more absurd. The men's hatred of the Corporal reaches a climax on Christmas Eve when, while they are intoxicated, they brutally kill him. The Corporal's death constitutes the drama's climax, at the end of Part One; thus the play's second half is a long anticlimax. The soldiers must now pay the consequences of their act, and they gradually discover that by killing the Corporal they have not liberated themselves, as they had thought, but have rather traded brutal oppression for degenerate anarchy. One by one they go to a fate which, although neither the Corporal's brutality nor death at the hands of the enemy, fulfills the original prophecy that they were a condemned squad.

One may question the accuracy of grouping *The Condemned Squad* with Sastre's dramas of social realism, for in this play one finds details of form and ideology characteristic of the dramas of frustration. The play's title, for example, implies a fatalism hardly compatible with the revolutionary ideology of Sastre's other social dramas—a fatalism tentatively confirmed in the drama itself.[4] The play's setting—World War Three, an anonymous location—is vague, somewhat fantastic, and strongly recalls the settings of Sastre's early experimental works. Characterization is sketchy and typal. However, *The Condemned Squad* differs in one very important respect from the dramas of frustration: it presents a world in which significant action is possible. By killing the Corporal the men manifest their ability to act and radically modify their situation, even though their act subsequently has ironic consequences. As in the rest of Sastre's social theater, the possibility and presence of action in the drama evoke an implicit commentary on man in the light of his social relations.

The Condemned Squad is thus characterized by a fundamental ambiguity which makes it possible to view this play as a bridge between the two major ideological tendencies of Sastre's work: paralysis and despair on the one hand, mobility and hope on the other.[5] This ambiguity pervades the play's dramatic structure, possible interpretations, and philosophical implications. It is an indication of Sastre's own ideological struggle and of his evolution. And most importantly, it gives *The Condemned Squad* a dramatic and ideological balance unequaled elsewhere in Sastre's theater.

The dramatic structure of *The Condemned Squad* is unusual, in that the drama's climax comes at the halfway point, rather than near the end of the play. A diagram of this structure would assume the form of a pyramid: the play's climactic (and only) act occurs at the end of Part One, as tensions culminate in the Corporal's murder. Part Two, on the other hand, consists of a movement away from action and toward final stagnation. Part One moves "up," from oppression (immobility) to liberation (action); Part Two moves "down," from action to renewed paralysis. The movement of Part One is positive; the movement of Part Two is negative. Dramatically, the end of Part Two is a recapitulation of the beginning of Part One: in both moments the soldiers are immobilized by their situation and are inferior to it.

This dramatic balance, a function of the play's fundamental ambiguity, permits complementary interpretations of *The Condemned Squad* in social, religious, existential, and metaphysical terms. Sastre's condemned squad is a metaphor of something much greater than itself, and the drama's richness and beauty are due to the varied interpretations which the anecdote permits—and, indeed, imposes. Philosophical suggestions rise abundantly and naturally from the plot, intertwining at many levels, complementing and enriching each other. It would be difficult not to see Corporal Goban as a symbol of militarism and tyranny, and his death as the rebellion of an oppressed collectivity. *The Condemned Squad* was, in fact, prohibited after only three performances in Madrid because military authorities saw the play as an attack on their profession.[6] Their perceptions were correct but incomplete. For although *The Condemned Squad* is undoubtedly a cry against the military mind and the stifled society it produces, it also examines the consequences of sudden, unilateral revolt. In this respect its revolutionary ideology is ambiguous; there is an implicit suggestion that one is no freer under anarchy than under tyranny.

In the throes of anarchy and degeneracy the men are haunted by the suspicion that what they have done will prove to be self-defeating. Referring to the murder of the Corporal, Andrés suggests that the men's salvation may have actually been the path they chose not to follow:

We've shut off our last escape. . . . Since all that happened, I've been thinking that maybe time would have passed and the offensive never would have come. . . . And in February maybe we would have been pulled out of here. . . . By then we would have lived out our punishment . . . maybe we would have been pardoned and sent back to our units, where we wouldn't have to put up with more danger than anybody else. . . . I've suddenly started thinking all this, now that it's too late. Now that our last escape has been shut off. (*OC*, 199-200)

The soldiers' revolt has led them to fates at least as bad as that which originally awaited them. Sastre's insistence on the relativity of revolutionary accomplishment is thus projected in the balanced form and ambiguous ideology of his play. *The Condemned Squad* is undoubtedly Sastre's best dramatic representation of the tension between order and anarchy, confidence and despair.

Critics have seen in *The Condemned Squad* an image of Europe's disillusioned postwar generation, which rather than being free of the terrors of war, finds itself faced with the atomic terror of the Cold War: a terror far greater than that of World War Two. At the time of the play's première Juan Emilio Aragonés saw its characters as "six provisional men, produced by this provisional Europe."[7] He called *The Condemned Squad* "a drama that provides no answers. A drama built on tragic, feverish questions. This is the drama of our disturbed, insecure Europe."[8] Ten years later he saw this play in essentially the same terms: "In *The Condemned Squad* we find, above all, a raw treatment of the provisional situation in which the youth of Europe has been living since 1946."[9] Ignacio Aldecoa, without confining his interpretation to postwar Europe, saw in Sastre's drama the anxiety and ambiguity of modern man:

Behind Alfonso Sastre's *Condemned Squad* lies the bittersweet fruit of our historical moment. The tragic sureness of catastrophe that we try not to think about, while the world moves ever closer to it; the uncertainty and despair of contemporary man, who at any moment may be sentenced to fall in and take his place in a condemned squad: there are the awesome suggestions with which Alfonso Sastre's play shakes our consciousness.[10]

The analogy between the condemned squad and modern man is supported both by Sastre and by the play's text. When his play was premièred in 1953 Sastre stated: "There is no point now in dreaming vaguely about a united Europe or about our participation in that phantasmal 'third world.' Caught in the middle, the youth of Europe work. They learn trades, take examinations, prepare themselves to be professors. What sense can all this possibly have under the threat of war? *The Condemned Squad* does not provide answers, but at least it probes the roots of some agonizing questions."[11] In the play itself Javier, the frightened intellectual, echoes Sastre's words: "A condemned squad. . . . We were already a condemned squad, even before the war broke out. A whole generation, stupidly condemned to the slaughterhouse. We studied, we worked, and we had already been assigned to a gigantic condemned squad" (*OC*, 190-91).

The relation between this analogy and the relative nature of political freedom is clear. One could paraphrase the play's implications by posing the question: What good did it do Europe to defeat Fascism, if the fruit of its victory was to be only a new and more terrible anxiety and enslavement? The ambiguity of this modern human situation gives *The Condemned Squad* its allegorical quality and lends a metaphysical resonance to the play's social statement. It is in this regard that the influence of Jean-Paul Sartre's *No Exit* is apparent. The initial entrapment of the soldiers, and their reactions to it, sharply recall those of Sartre's characters:

ANDRES. This is a trap. There's no way out of here. We don't have a chance.
JAVIER. You're right. This squad is condemned to death.
ANDRES. No . . . it's worse than that. We're condemned to *wait* for death. (*OC*, 177)

Pedro's observation suggests that their predicament is not unique, that it is shared by other men: "I tell you, there are a lot of squads like this, all along the front. Don't go thinking our situation is anything special" (*OC*, 177). But even though they share a common human destiny, they are alone:

JAVIER. . . . We're very far away . . .
PEDRO. Far from what?
JAVIER. I don't know . . . just far . . . (*OC*, 179)

Their only paths are "roads that don't go anywhere" and the most agonizing feature of their situation is the endless waiting. Their enemy is inscrutable, unpredictable, and deadly:

They are supposed to be fierce and cruel, but we don't know *how* fierce and cruel. . . . We can't pin them down, and that's what frightens us most. We know they don't think like we do . . . and that bothers us. . . . It disturbs us not to be able to measure them, reduce them to objects, grasp them with our minds. . . . They might do anything. . . . But *what?* What can we expect of them? If we knew we might be afraid. As it is, I'm not afraid. What I feel isn't fear. It's more like anguish. . . . There are worse things than dying in combat, you know. What really terrifies me now is the idea of being taken alive . . . because I can't imagine how they would kill me later. (*OC*, 178-79)

There emerges the clear image of a human condition in which man finds himself pursued, tormented, and condemned. Sastre's soldiers revolt against and destroy the apparent source of their misery, only to find that they must replace the Corporal's comforting absolutes with their own void: "You know, while he was alive we were almost happy. All we had to do was obey and suffer. We could all live with the illusion that we were being purified and that we might be saved. Each of us could remember his sin—a specific sin with date and details" (*OC*, 216). The Corporal thus projects the image of God, slain (abandoned) by a modern humanity which has been able to replace His tiring restrictions only with spiritual anarchy.[12] Like the characters of Sartre's *No Exit*, Javier reaches the conclusion that the whole catastrophe was diabolically preordained. But by whom? For what reason? We are again faced with the idea of man's anonymous transgression, later developed in *Drama and Society*: "Someone is punishing us for something . . . for something . . . I guess we must have committed some mistake back at the very beginning. . . . There's really no other explanation. A horrible, mysterious sin . . . and we don't know the slightest thing about it. Maybe a long time ago . . ." (*OC*, 217). In the play's final moment, when the young, sickly Luis asks for an explanation, Pedro's reply summarizes the ambiguity of man's existence:

LUIS. Pedro, why did all this happen? What did we do? What could we have ever done to deserve this? Do you think we deserved it, Pedro?

PEDRO. There's no point in asking. Why bother? Nobody will answer. (*Glances toward heaven.*) The only one who could tell you isn't talking. (*OC*, 220-21)

The specific human situation of *The Condemned Squad* thus points to the eternal human condition. At the play's end all characters are dead or lost except Pedro and Luis, who await the imminent arrival of a patrol that will take them back to civilization. One critic has suggested that these two characters do find salvation: Luis because by chance he was outside the cabin when the Corporal was murdered and will presumably not be punished, and Pedro because he has the strength of character to admit his guilt in the Corporal's death and accept the consequences of his act.[13] The idea is interesting, especially in view of the suggestion that Sastre may have wanted to leave open a faint possibility of hope for the European youth reflected in the play. But if these two soldiers have found salvation, it is only of the most relative sort. Luis has physically survived his immediate situation, but not through any form of self-assertion. He will continue to live, but Pedro accurately describes Luis's future life as "the long sentence that you have to live out . . ." (*OC*, 220). Even though he did not participate actively in the murder, his presence at the scene and his relationships with the other men have inevitably implicated him. On the one hand, his non-participation has deprived him of the satisfaction of having committed an authentic act; his fellow soldiers, even though burdened by the weight of responsibility, have found occasion to prove themselves free men, capable of acting upon their circumstances. Having acted, they have passed on to an existential realm from which Luis is excluded, and he longs to escape his loneliness by sharing in the consequences of the communal act: "No, Pedro, I don't want to keep living if all of you go away and leave me. There's no reason why I should be left out. Pedro, tell them I was with you that night! Tell them: Luis was in on it, too! Please tell them, Pedro!" (*OC*, 220) On the other hand, even though his life was not crystallized in a central act, Luis will forever be tormented by the ghost of his incidental involvement in the episode. The inception of his torment marks the beginning of his manhood, symbolized in the coming-of-age ceremony in the play's final scene:

PEDRO. Come on, boy. You're crying. There's no need to cry, you know. It's not worth it. (*Takes out a pack of cigarettes.*) Look. Two cigarettes left. Want one? (*Takes them out and crumples the pack.*)

LUIS. No. I've never smoked.

PEDRO. This can be your first time. (*They light up.*) Like it? (LUIS *nods, wiping away a tear, as if smoke had gotten in his eyes.* PEDRO *looks at him tenderly.*) Your first cigarette. . . . You'll never forget it. When this is all over and it all seems like a dream . . . and you can't quite recall how it was. . . . Years from now, if you want to remember me . . . all you'll have to do is light a cigarette . . . and its taste will bring back this hut . . . and we'll have just cut down Javier's body . . . and you'll see me here . . . looking at you . . . like this . . . (*Light fades.*) (*OC*, 221)

As for Pedro, his personal strength and positive attitude may have afforded him a certain Sartrian authenticity. But is his attitude really positive? Pedro's apparent courage becomes less convincing when one reflects that Pedro is a man who wants to die. His wife has been ravished by enemy soldiers, and it seems clear that returning home under existing circumstances would be a more terrible punishment for Pedro than would the firing squad that awaits him. Furthermore, in choosing to face a court martial, Pedro has opted to continue to act within the same framework of military values that had accounted for the squad's oppression under the Corporal. One may therefore question the extent to which Pedro has truly achieved authenticity by positing and acting upon his own values. One may be inclined to see Pedro as an excellent example of Sartrian "bad faith."

An individual's salvation can never be more than tentative and relative. And in oppressive situations it is seldom even that. This is the existential tragedy and the socialist imperative of *The Condemned Squad.*

* * * *

In many ways *The Gag* resembles *The Condemned Squad.* It is characterized by the same tightness of form and ideology, and the same allegorical quality. Isaías Krappo, who silences his family with violence and intimidation, recalls Corporal Goban. The family's revolt is analogous to that of the Corporal's soldiers. And *The Gag* projects the same rich, ambiguous ideological suggestions, although with an emphasis somewhat different from that of *The Condemned Squad.* Again, the transcendent implications are a natural product of the dramatic situation.

The central metaphor of this play is the gag (*mordaza*) of the title: the gag of fear that Isaías uses to keep his family from informing the police that he is the killer of a stranger whose body has been found on the Krappo property. Luisa, Isaías' daughter-in-law, was by chance a witness to the crime; thus Isaías' intimidation is initially directed at her. Even before the murder their relationship is tense, for old Isaías has an obvious lecherous interest in his son's pretty young wife. The personal dynamics among the characters thus exist primarily between Isaías and Luisa, and secondarily between Isaías and the rest of the family: his wife, Antonia, and his sons, Juan, Teo, and Jandro.

Since Luisa has been the only witness to Isaías' crime, she is the one who must first throw off the gag of fear with which Isaías has silenced her. She does this partially in the third scene by confiding to Teo and to her husband, Juan, that their father is the killer. She speaks in spite of Isaías' threat to kill her if she should ever reveal his guilt. However, the family's real liberation does not come until the sixth and final scene, for until that point Isaías succeeds in imposing on the entire family the gag of fear which he had first used to silence Luisa. In Scene vi it is again Luisa who takes the initiative, this time by informing the police inspector of Isaías' guilt. Isaías is arrested, and in the play's epilogue Juan returns from town with the news that his father has been killed while trying to escape from prison.

The social implications of *The Gag* are undeniable. Isaías can quite validly be taken as a symbol of oppression, general or specific. It is a bit confining to suggest, as one critic has done, that Isaías symbolizes capitalism and his family an oppressed humanity.[14] Also limited but somewhat more convincing is the interpretation of José María de Quinto, who directed the Madrid production of *The Gag.* Quinto sees the play's dramatic situation as an intentional image of Franco's Spain, and the "gag" as the limitations on free expression that prevail in Spain.[15] Sastre himself, without explicitly referring to Spain, has made it clear that he intended his play as a commentary on certain conditions which do indeed exist in that country: "It was my intention that the spectator perceive . . . the voice of my personal protest against certain conditions in which life is choked by a pressure dedicated to hiding truth."[16] The image of Spain, or of any country ruled by oppressive dictatorship, is sharpened by Luisa's key speech shortly before she decides to inform the inspector of Isaías' guilt:

"The house is quiet. You'd think nothing was happening here. You might even think we were all calm and happy. There are no unpleasantries, no shouts of desperation. . . . Nobody is angry or upset. So maybe it's true that nothing is happening. But then, that's strange, isn't it? Because we're all turning pale . . . and every day we grow sadder . . . calmer and sadder . . . because we can't live. This gag is choking us to death, and some day we'll have to speak. Some day we're going to scream out with whatever strength we have left. And on that day the blood will flow and the fury will be terrible." (*OC*, 326)

After the death of the tyrant the family breathes more easily; a sense of life and peace rises slowly from their mixed feelings of relief and sorrow. Juan senses the life blood that begins now to flow back into the family life: "And still, in spite of everything, how peaceful it is tonight. . . . We're calm, we're not weeping. . . . We may not want to admit it, but we feel good. The weather is clearing up . . . looks like it's going to be a good year. If this keeps up, the town will recover from all its troubles. We'll have fiestas like we used to. . . . I don't think we really need to be worried about the future" (*OC*, 342). Teo admonishes the family that, above all, one must live. Antonia says, "We have to keep on living . . ." (*OC*, 343). Isaías, like all oppressive forces, was evil because he prevented others from living, because he forced them to walk in fear, because he denied them the only dignity available to human beings. His subjects find life, freedom, and dignity only by asserting themselves in rebellion.

As in *The Condemned Squad*, however, the salvation is only relative. Luisa, and to a lesser extent Juan and Teo, have acted to secure their freedom and dignity, but their victory has not been absolute. Despite the sense of relief after Isaías' death, the family is bothered by doubts, by feelings of guilt for its part in his death. Juan sees that these doubts will always be with them: "What if he died suffering because of us, desperate and sad because his children turned him over to the police without shedding one single tear? How do we know what he was thinking there at the very end? We'll have this on our minds for the rest of our lives, and we'll never know for sure, and we'll never really be happy" (*OC*, 341-42). Teo sees the family's remorse as a punishment which Isaías has cunningly left them as his way of gaining revenge: "He's gotten even with us! Don't you see, he didn't want to escape! He knew full well he couldn't get away. And don't think he made a break for it because he had lost his mind, either. He did it for only one reason: to get revenge on us. He took off running so that the guards would have to kill him right there and then. He did it to horrify us . . . he did it so we would have these memories for the rest of our lives . . ." (*OC*, 341).

If Teo's theory is correct, the Krappo family has fallen into the same sort of trap that befell the members of Corporal Goban's condemned squad: they found themselves in a situation which demanded that they act or be enslaved, but having acted they discover that the price of action is loss of tranquillity. The metaphysical overtones of *The Gag* are less insistent than are those of *The Condemned Squad*, but in both these works one detects the same relationship between man and his condition, situation, and acts.

Whatever ideological suggestions one may find in *The Gag*, there is no doubt that they, along with the work's dramatic tension, are strengthened by Sastre's integrity of presentation. The final sense of freedom tempered by a new entrapment is consistent with the ambiguity that pervades the entire play. It is significant that the gag is a complex structure: fear of physical harm is only one of the pressures that silence Luisa and Isaías' sons. There are also other, more subtle factors. Furthermore, Sastre does not vilify Isaías; on the contrary, in many respects one tends to sympathize with Isaías and his situation. He has an exciting personal spontaneity and lust for life that keep his lecherous tendencies toward Luisa from becoming totally repugnant to the audience. At the end of the sixth scene the sexual motif reaches its climax when Isaías seizes Luisa passionately after she has denounced him to the police; at this point one realizes that his desire for Luisa is only a ramification of his desperate love of youth and life.

Moreover, although Isaías is guilty of murder, his culpability is highly relative. The man he killed had threatened to kill him and had furthermore been a collaborator during the French occupation. Isaías had fought with the Resistance—certainly, in Sastre's mind, the more admirable side of the conflict—and had committed atrocities against the stranger's family. After his arrest, Isaías himself notes the relativity of social guilt by observing that only a few years ago he and the inspector, now enemies, were comrades in battle. His murder of the stranger constitutes "guilt" only because circumstances have changed: "If I had killed that guy four years ago, you would have been happy about it and I would have been a hero . . . instead of just a murderer. . . . Maybe there's not much difference between a hero and a murderer. . . . It's not *who* you kill; it's when and how you kill him" (*OC*, 335). One cannot deny that Isaías is guilty not only of murder, but also of brutality and tyranny. But his family, which is led to freedom only through Luisa's initiative, is guilty of silence and acquiescence. Again, Sastre has heightened the investigative, agitational quality of his drama by invoking an ambiguous assignment of guilt.

Death in the Neighborhood and *Death Thrust* are two more of Sastre's very good dramas which deal with personal revolt but not social revolution. Sastre's concerns in these works are social, in that they involve the treatment of some men at the hands of others, but their political commentary is only implied. They are essentially investigations of certain social injustices—their nature, their effects, and their possible remedies. Both these plays are conceived primarily as social documents, but the perspective clearly relates social conditions to their existential context: oppression is evil because it negates human dignity. Freedom is the task of those who would salvage something of their lives in the face of an ultimate and sure oppression of a different nature.

In the prologue to *Death in the Neighborhood* the plot of the play is quickly revealed through dialogue between Pedro, a neighborhood bartender, and a police inspector. A child is struck by a car in the working-class neighborhood. Some local residents rush him to the clinic. Dr. Sanjo, who is supposed to be on duty, is absent and the child dies from lack of treatment. The following Sunday evening Dr. Sanjo comes into the "Bar Moderno" and finds himself greeted by the hostility of the local people gathered there. The tension mounts, violence erupts, and the doctor tries to escape. The crowd blocks his exit and kills him.

The epilogue also takes place in the bar and consists of a

dialogue in which the inspector attempts to obtain from Pedro information about the killing. The main body of the play develops a local color atmosphere, introduces characters, explores the background of the killing, and articulates some moral questions of a social nature. The theme of social irresponsibility—a source of social injustice—is central to the play's ideology. Legally, Pedro and his accomplices are guilty of murder. But again Sastre mitigates their real guilt with suggestions of its relative nature. Dr. Sanjo's irresponsibility emerges as an aspect of a larger social injustice to which the working people are subject. For those people the doctor's behavior becomes symbolic of a social and legal system which, from the viewpoint of the poor, is criminally inadequate. Were they thus not justified in taking the law into their own hands? There is a clear implication that they were, for the constituted system deprived them of dignity and even life. The inspector even suggests that there is something admirable about the fact that these people have not been totally stupefied by oppression and that they still have the capacity to rebel:

> You know, murder today isn't what it used to be. Today murder is carried out, you might even say, gently. . . . The killers are sitting behind desks. They sign a paper, give an order. . . . They don't have to wrinkle their suits, and at night they go home and kiss the wife and kids. Nothing has happened. They're not murderers. . . . But those people that killed that man in here, that's a different matter. When they went home that night their clothes were torn, their faces were scratched, their eyes had a cold stare. . . . And as soon as they walked in the house, their wives and kids knew they had killed a man. (*OC*, 537)

Consciously or otherwise, Sastre has also mitigated the killers' guilt in a purely theatrical way. The frequently lyrical rhythm of the dialogue, the "coincidences" which bring Dr. Sanjo and his killers to the bar at the same time, and the ritualistic nature of his execution all project a suggestion of fatalism in his death. Of course, there is a fundamental philosophical contradiction between the work of fate and the free acts of men. But in a purely theatrical sense the effect of these elements on the audience would probably be to create a sense of justification for the killing by reducing any appearance of arbitrariness on the part of those who commit this act of violence.

As usual, Sastre does not create a totally reprehensible antagonist. There are reasons for Sanjo's chronic irresponsibility:

Sometimes I have these attacks and I have to get out of the clinic. . . . I feel suffocated in there. . . . You know what I mean, don't you? I feel . . . I feel afraid! It horrifies me to be on duty! Do you know what it's like, waiting there, all locked up? Waiting, without knowing what you're waiting for? *Anything* might come through that door! A man with his head broken open. . . . Blood. . . . I never wanted to work in the clinic in the first place. I wanted to do research. But I needed the money. I had to eat. . . . So I ended up in that hospital and I started drinking . . . (*OC*, 580-81)

As Leonard C. Pronko has noted, "Although the irresponsible doctor is despicable, he is not presented as devoid of humanity."[17] In his own way, he too has been a victim of unjust economic pressures. Sastre allows the audience to glimpse the doctor's individual life and to perceive its relation to his social life. Dr. Sanjo has been unable to reconcile the two and this failure leads to his death. By revealing a previously concealed side of the doctor, Sastre gives the play's climactic scene a greater dramatic validity.

The theme of *Death Thrust* is exploitation—by a specific man in a dramatic situation, but implicitly on a larger scale as well. The principal characters are José Alba, a bullfighter, and Juan Marcos, his manager. That *Death Thrust* is not concerned with the art of killing bulls should be obvious to anyone who reads it or sees it performed.[18] One can perhaps see in this drama a certain iconoclastic intent, a desire to dismantle the Spanish myth of the glamorous and superhuman bullfighter.[19] But even this element is secondary, for the ideological essence and dramatic tension of *Death Thrust* rest in the special relationship between the principal characters: Marcos, egoistic and possessive, and Alba, dependent and exploited.

The form of this play resembles that of *Death in the Neighborhood*. The prologue and epilogue are temporally and spatially set apart from the work's body. Marcos' character, his relation to Alba, and the drama's denouement are revealed in the prologue; having aborted the suspense factor at an early moment, Sastre can then dedicate himself to an investigation of details and causes. This task involves an intensive examination of the relationship between Marcos and Alba.

As we learn in the prologue, Marcos is notorious in professional circles. He specializes in converting young aspirants into famous bullfighters, but his price is high. He wishes not only to be a manager but also a creator. He demands total sacrifice and total submission from his creatures. They become famous while he gratifies his ego by dominating and humiliating another human being. If his victims refuse to become totally dependent on him or if they break under the strain of his demands, Marcos readily discards them. After all, Spain is full of hungry, naïve young men who will pay any price to achieve fame and escape hunger. His obsessive need for absolute possession of the men he manages acquires a horrible magnificence on the stage, for Marcos is not a stereotype or an inhuman villain. "He is not a simple, commonplace cynic, but rather a blind force that assumes form on the stage by carrying out its own peculiar, inevitable destiny. The implacable character of the manager achieves grandeur, in spite of his cruelty."[20] Marcos' defense of his possessiveness is cruel but plausible:

> I can't do anything with just a little bit. . . . I need a whole man. I can't share him with a woman or with anyone. It sounds ugly, doesn't it? But there've been enough women in my life, so you won't misunderstand. Bulls are that way. . . . You have to give them free men, ready for anything. . . . It's from those men the great figures come. What can come from happy family life? A brilliant diplomat, perhaps. But bullfighters, no! Nor artists either! Nothing important! They're a world apart. Made of other clay, and it's a pity to throw them away.[21]

Marcos' psychology is well developed. Whatever the past experience that has produced his present character, he is portrayed in terms of his relations with others and consequently acquires shading and convincingness. He forces his creatures to be emotionally and practically dependent on him because his own self-esteem depends on his ability to possess others. In order to believe in his own existence he must feed on the dignity of others; he must humiliate them and make them appendages of himself. Thus Marcos, in a sense, is emotionally dependent on those to whom he attaches himself. When his bullfighters fall he feels humiliated; when they are afraid he is ashamed; when they laugh he is happy. This mutual dependency of the two principal characters contributes to a definition of each, and to the drama's tension and coherence.

The relationship between Marcos and Alba is best defined in

Act Two, as Alba prepares for the bullfight that will prove to be his last. Marcos' hold on Alba has been momentarily loosened by the unexpected arrival of Alba's estranged wife, Gabriela. She and Marcos are enemies, for they both seek to possess José Alba. Gabriela perceptively describes Marcos' aspirations in terms which point to the sexual overtones present in his feelings toward Alba: "I'll tell you what he wants! He wants everything! He wants you to belong to him, body and soul! Yes, that's exactly what he wants, and I don't care how it sounds! He wants you like a woman, more than a woman, because he can't even stand the idea of sharing your life with anyone! That's why he separated us before!" (p. 252). After Gabriela's exit, Marcos seeks to terrify Alba in order to regain his dominance. He calmly and cruelly manipulates Alba's emotions, and Alba projects the image of a young virgin, terrified and fascinated by her seducer:

JOSÉ. . . . What are you going to do with me?
MARCOS. What am I going to do? Nothing.
JOSÉ. I'm afraid.
MARCOS. I'm used to that. It's a humiliation I've had to get used to.
JOSÉ. (*Looking at him horrified.*) I'm frightened . . . of you.
MARCOS. (*Laughs bitterly.*) Of me? What for?
JOSÉ. Don't do anything to me, Marcos.
MARCOS. Me?
JOSÉ. Help me.
MARCOS. To what?
JOSÉ. To get through it. Without you, I can't.
MARCOS. (*Irritated.*) Now you remember.
JOSÉ. I'm . . . alone . . . sick . . . I feel . . . (*Hand to back of neck*) a pressure here . . . (p. 258)

As Marcos threatens to withdraw his support, Alba's need for it grows stronger:

MARCOS. . . . Call your wife, if you want.
JOSÉ. My wife?
MARCOS. She'll help you. (JOSÉ *shakes his head despairingly.*)
JOSÉ. Talk to me like you always do. Tell me . . .
MARCOS. No. (*He continues eating. He looks at* JOSÉ *with an almost mocking expression.*)
JOSÉ. Then?
MARCOS. Then, get ready. It's almost time.
JOSÉ. I'm (*He shudders.*) ready.

MARCOS. If the wind keeps up, be careful.
JOSÉ. Is it very windy?
MARCOS. Quite.
JOSÉ. I'm afraid of the wind.
MARCOS. Get your bearings from the flag. Stick to the most sheltered section of the ring. (*Eats.*)
JOSÉ. You'll be there, as usual?
MARCOS. I'll try to be there. If nothing unforeseen comes up.
JOSÉ. What could come up? (MARCOS *has stopped eating. He lights a cigarette.*)
MARCOS. I don't know. Something.
JOSÉ. You're going to leave me alone?
MARCOS. You don't need me any longer. You know all you need to know.
JOSÉ. Don't leave the edge of the bullring! I want to feel you're there.
MARCOS. Only if it rains too hard.
JOSÉ. Even if it rains! Stay there!
MARCOS. Don't be a child, José. Leave me in peace. (pp. 259-60)

Later, however, Alba shows that their roles can be reversed, that Marcos is potentially as dependent on Alba's whims as Alba is on those of Marcos:

MARCOS. . . . You're going to fight knee-deep in the mud . . . and against bulls as big as hell itself! Now you know the truth!
JOSÉ. And you can tell it to me that way? As coldly as that? (MARCOS *shrugs his shoulders.* JOSÉ *picks up a knife from the table.*) You're blurry. . . . I can hardly see you. As though I were going to pass out.
MARCOS. (*Frightened.*) Drop that!
JOSÉ. (*With a confused smile.*) No.
MARCOS. Drop it, I tell you!
JOSÉ. As though I were going to faint! (*He takes a step toward* MARCOS, *who is frightened.*)
MARCOS. Drop it, or I'll make you drop it. (pp. 261-62)

In desperation Alba plunges the knife into his abdomen, impulsively assuming that he cannot go through with the fight if he is wounded. A doctor comes and applies a temporary bandage but warns that any abrupt movement could produce a dangerous hemorrhage. So great is Marcos' desire not to be humiliated and so slight is his concern for Alba as a human being, that he readily agrees to let his protégé perform in spite of his dangerous condition. Alba himself makes the decision to face the bulls; he would rather risk his life than be scorned by Marcos. The consequence is that predicted by the doctor: although Alba is gored slightly, he dies not of the goring but of a loss of blood from the knife wound.

The complex, tense nature of this personal drama gives vitality to the social commentary implicit in *Death Thrust.* Sastre has spoken of this play in its relation to the myth of Saturn, who devoured his sons. He describes Saturn as "someone whose survival depends on the destruction of his creations. I find this myth unfortunately alive in the society in whose breast we scurry and struggle."[22] Even without Sastre's help, the attentive reader or spectator perceives this anthropophagic image in *Death Thrust*: in the prologue Dr. Sánchez compares Marcos to Saturn, and in Act One Alba calls Marcos a "hairy, old spider" (p. 234). As a specific social analogy one may suggest modern materialism, or capitalism. Sastre's reason for entitling the play *Death Thrust,* even though Alba does not die of a goring, is interesting in this regard. The thrust, or *cornada,* in question is the *cornada del hambre* (thrust of hunger) which drives men to let themselves be exploited and become the mistresses of men like Juan Marcos.[23] Sastre's suggestion is that there is something quite ill about a society that is divided into managers and protégés.

The epilogue of *Death Thrust* has been frequently criticized as superfluous and strained.[24] This criticism would seem to be unjust, for the epilogue does in fact have the important function of sharpening the play's ideological postulates by providing a counterexample for José Alba. After Alba's death Marcos calls on Rafael Pastor, a humble tavernkeeper who had been Alba's understudy on the day of his death. Marcos has decided that Pastor is to be his next creation. However, he is mistaken. Pastor rejects his temptations, realizing that Marcos is actually asking him to prostitute his humanity: "I don't know what you call people like me. But I do know, from what I've seen already, that there are people in this life who live off the misfortunes of other people's danger, of other's [sic] deaths . . . of the slow wasting away of others. . . . That's a typical Spanish story, too, isn't it?" (p. 272). A minor character thus becomes the vehicle for the play's explicit ideological statement by emerging as a man strong enough to salvage his dignity from the degrading cycle of need and exploitation. In this way he lends perspective to José Alba's defeat and clarity to the main body of the drama.

III *Dramas of Revolution*

Pathetic Prologue, The Red Earth, and *In the Net* deal directly with three distinct aspects of the revolutionary process. The "pathetic prologue" is the terrorism which the Communist Party views as the necessary prelude to political revolution.[25] The play's theme is the moral ambiguity of revolutionary violence and Sastre has referred to *Pathetic Prologue* as a "play that attempts to achieve a balance between the personal morality of the character, and political effectiveness. . . ."[26] The play is marred by melodrama and sentimentality, but these defects become minor in view of the validity of the moral issue and the force of its presentation.

Can one justify the killing of innocent people with a terrorism whose ultimate aim is a greater degree of social justice for all? This is the question that torments Antón and Oscar, two young members of a terrorist group. Antón is especially bothered by the vague and anonymous nature of the work he is ordered to carry out: "All I ask is to be allowed to shoot at somebody in particular. Throwing a bomb into the streets is something so vague, it frightens me, like the dark used to frighten me when I was a kid. . . . I see now that the death we deal out is pure accident. . . . It's nothing. . . . We can't hold on to it. . . . It evaporates right between our fingers. I wanted to be responsible for something definite, exact, even if it was just the death of a child" (*OC,* 66-67).[27] His inability to reconcile scruples with what the Party considers political necessity leads to his suicide. Oscar, mistakenly believing that his own terrorism has caused the death of his brother, rebels against the organization's inhumanity and announces that he is taking command of the group:

> "I plan to reorganize it myself and send it out to work independently. This group is going to do things my way. We'll go to the heart of the matter. The people who die will die because they have to. We want concrete action, not vague terrorism. Nobody is going to die unnecessarily. And we're going to know beforehand who the victims will be. We'll use a pistol: one clean shot to bring down the man who truly cannot be allowed to live. From now on I intend to have at least the nobility and dignity of a gangster." (*OC,* 94)

The dilemma is not merely an abstract moral conflict. For Oscar it attains existential significance: in order to justify one's existence it is necessary to justify one's acts, and Oscar is not at all convinced that his acts are justified. Thus, Sastre again achieves a merger of existential and social crises. One is reminded of Hugo Barine, the young protagonist of Sartre's *The Dirty Hands,* as Oscar futilely seeks self-justification in a series of acts and finally discovers it in a suicidal move in the play's final scene. He decides not to flee the police who are coming for him. In this way, he feels, he will give to his life and past actions the meaning which they lack:

Now I know that I can still do something important for the cause: I can suffer for it. I'll make myself useful to the cause by *suffering* . . . , by standing up to their torture in that filthy basement until they finally say: 'This is useless. This Party is more than we can cope with. Its men just let themselves be killed without ever opening their mouths.' That's where I belong: down there in that dark basement. I'm ready for the police! Let them come and carry me away! They can beat my body to a pulp, they can burn my hands, and I'll shout 'Long live the Revolution!' I'll shout it until my face is just a bloody mass. And then whatever is left of me will be a man again. (*OC,* 105)

Pathetic Prologue was Sastre's first play which dealt directly with the theme of social revolution and its moral complexities. His earlier works had been imbued with an awareness of injustice in the world, but only in a vague, moralistic way. During the 1940's he had an awareness of injustice but little hope for its elimination; his attitude was a "nihilistic moralism." In a later reference to his play *Uranium 235* Sastre wrote: ". . . in the face of a possible atomic catastrophe I offered only a weak protest and could recommend only that the survivors (if there were any) start over again and rebuild the world."[28] *Pathetic Prologue* thus marks Sastre's "new awareness of the theater as a social function."[29] In this drama he found himself faced with an eternal moral dilemma, and only after several years of vacillation did he finally give this conflict a definitive resolution.[30] Rather than let himself be paralyzed by the moral ambiguity of action, Sastre suggests through Oscar that there is no choice but to accept the death of the innocent if it is indispensable to revolutionary progress.[31] If men had followed the dictates of Christianity, revolution would not be necessary. The fact that it *is* necessary, however, means that scruples must be momentarily sacrificed.[32]

Even though this ideological conclusion is hesitant, it is significant that Sastre chose to apply it to *Pathetic Prologue,* for it is also implicit in his later dramas of revolution. *The Red Earth* and *In the Net* are not concerned with the moral ambiguity of revolution; in these dramas, the question is no longer whether revolution is morally justified, but simply how it is to be carried out. There is no suggestion that all revolutionary activity is automatically justified, or that moral uncertainties disappear as soon as one begins to fight against social injustice. The preface to *Four Dramas of Revolution* is testimony to Sastre's continuing awareness of these ambiguities. But the ambiguity so essential to *Community Bread, Pathetic Prologue, The Condemned Squad,* and *The Gag* is not dominant in the later dramas of revolution. A revolution is tragic in any case, but the suggestion of Sastre's more mature theater is that it is a tragedy that must be endured if man is to combat the other tragedy of modern life: social injustice.

The Red Earth examines the efficacy of collective action as a means of combating exploitation. In this work, as in *In the Net,* Sastre focuses on the fraternity of mass effort, thus posing a sharp contrast to the tragic loneliness which the characters of some other plays must suffer. Pablo, a young idealist, comes to work in the coal mines and discovers what everyone else there already knows: the miners are exploited and degraded. They have no dignity, no chance for self-realization; they are merely objects in the hands of the powerful few who control the enterprises for which they work. Strikes and rebellions have been attempted in the past, but they have apparently been inconsequential.

The specific injustice that arouses Pablo's indignation is the way in which the miners are evicted from their company-owned houses when they reach retirement age. They are turned out into the world with no pension, no shelter, and nothing to show for their many years in the service of the company. Thus, when Pablo meets Pedro and his daughter, Inés, who are to be evicted the following day, he says, as men have said before him, "Somebody ought to do something . . ." (*OC,* 355). Pablo's youth and lack of familiarity with the system allow him to doubt the inevitability of this injustice:

PABLO. . . . I don't understand.
INÉS. What don't you understand?
PABLO. I don't understand why there's not the slightest angry

reaction when this moment finally comes, when they throw a miner out of his house. This afternoon the fellows were talking sadly about the fact that old Pedro is leaving. But that's all they were doing—talking about it sadly—as if nothing could be done.

INÉS. Nothing *can* be done, and you may as well forget it. (*OC*, 353-54)

Pablo challenges his comrades and Sastre challenges his audience:

PABLO. You people don't even remember how to react to an injustice.

OLD MAN. Life has kicked us around pretty hard, boy. . . . We figure it's better not to react too much. (*OC*, 366)

Pablo succeeds in convincing his comrades to strike the next morning. They gather in front of Pedro's house at dawn, with the hope of preventing his departure. Violence ensues and several company officials and miners are killed.

The fifth scene is an imitation of the famous investigation scene of Lope de Vega's *Fuenteovejuna.* One by one the miners are tortured by the police, and unanimously they insist that the violence was planned and carried out by the entire community. But the investigation does not end like that of *Fuenteovejuna.* Angered by the miners' refusal to identify the instigators, the police captain orders his men to machine-gun the entire mining community. The miners will pay for their action with the blood of their wives and children.

In the play's final scene (the second scene of a divided epilogue), Pablo finds himself in a situation identical to that of Pedro when Pablo first came to the mines. Now an old man and married to Inés, Pablo has reached retirement age and is preparing to abandon his house. This scene appears at first to be a repetition of the play's opening scene, but it differs in one important respect: one now sees that the efforts made by Pablo and others to secure a better life for the miners have apparently achieved some degree of success. The process has been long and painful and much work remains to be done, but the suffering of the past has not been in vain. The young man who calls on Pablo convinces him that struggle is not futile, just as Pablo, in his youth, had convinced others:

YOUNG MAN. But now it's different. Now we have comrades. You're not going to leave here.

PABLO. . . . You listen to me, boy. We've been through all that before, and we're not about to start it again. It was bloody . . . it was useless . . . and it was so terrible that there are still nights when I can't sleep for thinking about it . . . (*Hides his face in his hands and murmurs:*) And it was all for nothing.

YOUNG MAN. (*Enthusiastically.*) No, Sr. Pablo, it wasn't all for nothing! It was so that tonight I could come here and tell you that things are different now! It was so I could tell you that if the blood of the miners is ever shed again, that bloodshed will be felt all over the country. Thousands of workers you don't even know would walk out of the factories. The news would reach the countryside, and the farmers would stop their work and turn their faces toward the mines. And the students would take to the streets and stand up to the police to demand that justice be done. And a lot of smug people would turn white with fear.

PABLO. (*A strange look on his face.*) You may be right. (*OC*, 408)

The progress of the workers does not signify only material gains. For Pablo it means above all that his responsibility in the massacre of the town many years ago has been justified. If no good had come from that atrocity, his silence before the police would have amounted only to a hideous caprice. The hopeful ending of *The Red Earth* clearly implies that Pablo and the others were justified in their intransigence. For the workers in general, better living conditions mean a greater degree of dignity for them as human beings. Early in the play Pedro had poignantly lamented to his wife: "So many years of suffering. . . . Little bits of happiness . . . little moments of love . . . and none of it has left a mark in the earth. That's the way we poor people live. And that's the way we die and disappear . . ." (*OC*, 361). An oppressive economic system prevents man's self-realization as a human being; it reduces him to insignificance among the creatures and things of the world. The existential and social evils of such a system are inseparable. Humanity's task must be the establishment of a society which will allow every man to leave "a mark in the earth."

In the Net is the best of Sastre's dramas of revolution. In this tense, unified drama Sastre examines "the human condition of the 'clandestine man'": the revolutionary activist who is forced to flee, hide, and live on the margin of humanity.[33] The characters of *In the Net* are Algerian nationalists who are hiding from a police roundup in a small oppressive apartment. Some observers have criticized Sastre for showing only one side of the Algerian conflict: that of the nationalists.[34] It is true that the play dwells at length on the terror and atrocities of the police against the rebels and does not suggest that the rebels may likewise have been guilty of atrocities. This fact, however, is of little or no significance, and it certainly does not compromise the play's ideological integrity. The identity of the warring factions of *In the Net* is almost irrelevant. There are no specific allusions to the Algerian war as such, and except for the delicacy of the issue at the time of the play's première, the identity of the warring parties would probably have been of little interest. The author's sympathies, as always, are evidently with those who fight against colonialism, and he appears to have reconciled himself to the inevitable moral ambiguities of revolution, but *In the Net* was not written with the intent of exalting the Algerian nationalists and maligning the colonialists. This drama focuses rather on the effect which revolutionary activity has on those who dedicate themselves to it. The effects of this activity on the characters of *In the Net* result from conditions under which all revolutionary activism must transpire. The revelation of these conditions makes *In the Net* a continuation of Sastre's "theater conceived as a form of struggle and investigation of reality."[35]

The prime condition of the revolutionary is that he is pursued. His continued existence can be secured only through secrecy and flight; he thus becomes a "clandestine man." This condition, as lived by Sastre's characters, leads to a reduction or loss of one's humanity. Paradoxically, the characters act in fraternity but are forced to live in isolation—from the world and from each other. Tenderness and trust are luxuries which these revolutionaries cannot afford. Celia states tersely, "The less we know about each other, the better" (*OC*, 803). Celia, Leo, and Teyeb suspect Pablo of being a policeman who has infiltrated their group. Celia allows her lover, Leo, to be captured and tortured because warning him of the roundup would involve risks; their situation has rendered human contact impossible: "The area had been roped off by the police. No one could go in or out. I was so near you, and yet you might as well have been in another world" (*OC*, 829). When Leo makes his way painfully to the hideout after his release, Celia overlooks the fact that he is in great pain and reprimands him for taking the risk of coming there. Leo cannot even enjoy the solace of silent shame after giving information to the police under stress of torture; he must tell Pablo the details of his torture and confession so that an effort can be made to save those comrades he has implicated:

LEO. . . . I'm so ashamed . . .
PABLO. Forget about your shame. That's a luxury we can't afford right now. Go on: tell us everything, just as it happened. (*OC*, 834)

In addition to being forced into isolation and harshness, the clandestine man loses his humanity in a more general way: he forfeits his capacity for dignity and self-assertion. Celia explains to Pablo in Act One: ". . . this is our pitiful heroism: we pretend we don't exist" (*OC*, 808). Tayeb is sensitive to the necessity of constantly running and the impossibility of finding tranquillity and emotional stability. The greatest indignity is that which Leo has suffered at the hands of the police. During Leo's long, horrifying account of his torture, the spectator realizes that the sadistic police have done more than break their victim's body.[36] They have destroyed his dignity as a man, and he will never again be able to walk upright, free of shame and fear. When Leo pathetically admits shame, cowardice, and "lack of dignity," he is referring to his weakness in having given information to the police. The fundamental source of his indignity, however, is not his confession, but the fact of his torture. During his ordeal his humiliation has reached an absolute degree: it has deprived him of the sureness of his own identity and existence: "I screamed . . . and the scream seemed to come from someone else. Then they gave me another shock, and another! Convulsions. . . . My voice sounded strange. Like it wasn't even mine . . ." (*OC*, 836). He has left the police station a broken, useless human being. His only fitting end is a desperate, suicidal flight when the police finally invade the apartment.

In the Net is an effective piece of theater because its form and dramatic devices so strongly support the dramatic situation. Sastre has observed the classical unities of time, place and action; the resultant tightness of construction parallels the inherent tension of the characters' situation. The apartment which serves as a hideout is hot, cramped, and suffocating—like the situation of its inhabitants. There is an obvious double meaning in Pablo's frequent complaint that he can hardly breathe in the apartment.

Like the people in it, the apartment is relatively isolated. It is reached by an elevator whose approach is marked by a noise quite audible to the audience. The motif of this sound becomes an effective source of tension, for it signifies the possible arrival of the police, whose sudden intrusion is a constant threat. The uncertainty and mistrust in which the characters live is extended to the audience by Pablo's suspicious behavior and by the unresolved riddle of the identity of the group's leader. The dynamics of the drama are the natural consequences of the personal tensions experienced by the characters; a tense restraint is characteristic of the dialogue, but it is sharply broken by emotional outbursts three times before the play's critical moment at the end of Act Two.[37] Late in the final act, Leo suffers a nervous breakdown simultaneously with the alarm signal which indicates that the police have actually arrived.

Like most of Sastre's plays, *In the Net* has its ambiguities. These do not concern the moral justification of the revolutionary efforts in progress, but rather their effectiveness. At the play's end, Leo is dead, and Celia and Pablo have been taken away to the torture chamber. Does *In the Net*, then, provide the element of hope which Sastre considers essential to effective social drama? And do the characters break out of their situation and triumph over it, or does it prove stronger than they? One may cautiously reply that *In the Net* does have a hopeful ending, that the positive attitude of Celia and Pablo does hint at the success of the revolution, and consequently at the triumphant self-assertion of the characters. However, this eventuality depends on the ability of Celia and Pablo to resist the torture that awaits them. Thus, even if they and the revolution triumph, the victory will have been won at the expense of physical and emotional integrity. Like Sastre's other dramas of revolution, *In the Net* offers a glimpse of a better world that can be attained only at a price which few are willing to pay.

These ambiguities are built into the drama's form. In the context of a tight structural unity, Sastre gives *In the Net* an ending which avoids a total cathartic effect, thus stamping the play's ideological ambiguities on the spectator's emotional reactions. The open-ended nature of the denouement suggests neither total tragedy nor sure triumph. The final line of dialogue —"Murderers"—is spoken by the Arabic janitor after he has discovered Leo's body. It is directed at the audience, rather than being simply a final touch to the illusion of reality that has transpired on the stage. It thus produces a jolting stylistic break with the rest of the play. The effect of the ending, in a well-staged performance, would be to counteract the hypnotic effect of audience empathy. The overall effect of the play would be to involve the spectator emotionally, but without immobilizing his mind. In Sastre's words, *In the Net* should "produce in the spectators that awareness which, going beyond an immediate cathartic effect, is the ultimate goal of theater conceived as struggle and investigation" (*OC*, 796). *In the Net,* and Sastre's explanation of it, illustrate and summarize the agitational intent of Sastre's penetrative social realism.

CHAPTER 7

The Epic Phase

I *Sastre and Brecht*

IN 1960 Sastre published the first of several essays devoted to an analysis and criticism of the "epic" theater of Bertolt Brecht. Sastre found his Aristotelian principles in conflict with the theater prescribed and practiced by the great German theater man, and while reacting favorably to Brecht's revolutionary intent he expressed some strong reservations about the efficacy of his dramatic forms and techniques:

> I, too, want the theater to avoid "magic" and I want it to concern itself with something other than the creation of a naturalistic illusion. But it seems to me that Brecht's criticism is based on a pseudoproblem, or at least on a problem of doubtful gravity. I personally find that Brecht's demands are already met by the "dramatic" theater: distantiation, criticism, and all the rest. And in the "epic" theater I see the danger that as the distances grow longer, the spectator will lose sight of us, and we will lose sight of him.[1]

During the following years, however, Sastre became more aware of Brecht's immeasurable impact on the modern theater, and of the fact that the theater's historical development had been essentially a dialectical, rather than a linear, process. His attitude toward Brecht thus underwent modification. In 1963, reversing his earlier position, Sastre wrote: ". . . I see that a modern *Poetics* for the theater must take the form of a negation of Brecht's negation of the Aristotelian drama, and can never be a reaffirmation of the latter in the face of Brecht's criticism" (*AR*, 8). Rather than continue to resist Brechtianism on the basis of Aristotelian principles, Sastre now proposed a new theater derived from Brecht's experiments, but surpassing them. Brecht had been of monumental importance in determining the directions of the twentieth-century theater and the Brechtian theater must be the point of departure for further innovations. However, these must go beyond Brechtianism by seeking dramatic forms capable of providing a fusion between Brecht's discoveries and other experiences of the modern theater.

The evolution of Sastre's critical attitude toward Brecht parallels the evolution of his own dramatic forms. In his most recent plays Sastre has cultivated an "epic" theater, obviously inspired by Brecht, but seeking to transform Brecht's propaganda-ridden spectacle into a more profound vision of society and revolution.[2] Sastre's epic plays, like his dreams of social realism, suggest a revolutionary ideology. At times they do so directly, through themes and ideas, but more consistently and more importantly the revolutionary implications are conveyed through a skillful manipulation of dramatic form. In his epic plays Sastre relies more heavily on suggestion than on argumentation; he is more concerned with exposing the spectator to provocative images of revolution than with convincing him rationally of the urgency of transforming society. The underlying intent of Sastre's epic plays is to place before the spectator the image of a world that can be changed—a world in which cause-and-effect relationships are arbitrary and reality is fluid. To this end Sastre employs various techniques of distantiation, or alienation: dramatic devices designed to minimize spectator empathy by destroying the illusion of synthetic, naturalistic reality. Hopefully, the spectator will leave the theater with a heightened awareness of both the need and the possibility of social transformation.

The details of form characteristic of Sastre's epic plays can be summarized as follows:

(a) *Looseness of structure.* A large number of scenes and episodes are linked in a loose, frequently arbitrary manner. The "knots," to use Brecht's metaphor, are plainly visible to the audience; the result is a structure which gives the appearance of susceptibility to change, in contrast to the image of inevitability produced by a logical, Aristotelian structure. In the prefaces to his epic plays Sastre even goes so far as to grant the director explicit permission to modify the plays as he sees fit.

(b) *Narrative elements.* These take various forms: a speech delivered directly to the audience, "asides" which establish a supposedly private communication between the audience and one character, a ballad sung on stage, titles given to scenes, signs held up to announce in advance the developments about to transpire. The narrative elements have the function of creating the peculiar historical perspective of the epic theater, by producing the illusion that the events of the stage have already "happened" and are simply being recounted, in contrast to the naturalistic illusion of events presently transpiring before the spectator. Furthermore, by giving advance notice of the action about to take place, the narrative elements abort the suspense factor, thus reducing the danger of an hypnotic, immobilizing empathy on the part of the spectator.

(c) *Fusion of reality and pretense.* Spectators become actors, actors step out of character and chat intimately with the audience, action takes place in the aisles and lobby of the theater, the supposed author of a play appears as a character in the play, or the dialogue comments on the play being performed. Paradoxically, an aesthetic distance between spectator and spectacle is produced by removing the traditional separations between the two.

(d) *Unnerving sound, light, and visual effects.* The flow of the performance is punctuated by screams, sirens, raucous music, unexpected light changes, and scenes of sudden violence or grotesque ugliness. These are another of many devices to assure that the spectator is not lulled into unconsciousness by a palatable, predictable sequence of events.

(e) *Stylistic variety or incongruity.* This is a general feature of the epic theater and a fundamental technique of distantiation. Under this heading one could include countless stylistic details designed to undermine the spectator's persistent search for unity and logic in the spectatcle before him. Some examples found in Sastre's epic plays are unexpected obscenities in the dialogue, cinematic projections, incongruous bits of behavior by the characters, details of modern life or speech inserted into an historical context, highly stylized acting employed only at certain specified moments, and the use of music.

(f) *The familiar presented in a strange light.* One of Brecht's basic principles was that a play's situations and episodes should be recognizable to the audience, but that they should be presented in an unaccustomed manner, in order that the spectator be encouraged to view the world with a fresh, potentially revolutionary perspective. Sastre complies with this principle in various ways: through stylization (e.g., reality as seen through the mist of a dream), by suggesting mythic figures in his characters (e.g., Don Quixote and Sancho Panza in the persons of Miguel Servet and his friend, or Christ in the person of Miguel Servet), or by drawing obvious or subtle parallels between the fictional incidents of a play and contemporary realities familiar to the entire audience (e.g., allusions to Naziism, American imperialism, and the Franco regime).

II *Contemporary Epic Plays*

Nocturnal Assault, The Banquet, and *The Fantastic Tavern* have contemporary settings and themes. Like many of Sastre's earlier dramas, they do not deal directly with the revolutionary process, but are rather more concerned with illuminating certain problems and injustices resulting from the present imperfect society. *Nocturnal Assault* is Sastre's earliest epic experiment. Its composition in 1959 was the immediate result of his new interest in the Brechtian theater. With regard to its date of composition and the details of its form, *Nocturnal Assault* is no more than a precursor to Sastre's epic phase. It is, in fact, a relatively unimportant piece of work, suffering from the same imbalance characteristic of the less successful dramas of social realism. In this play Sastre obviously intended a parallel between the terrible suspense of a personal vendetta and the general anxiety of an atomic age whose creatures live with the constant threat of mass destruction. However, the analogy is not embodied in the play's action, but rather in an essentially unrelated and somewhat distracting narration which periodically reminds the audience of the militarism and atomic terror that threaten its life.

The Banquet recalls *Death Thrust* in its exposé of behind-the-scenes exploitation of celebrities—in this case, movie actors and actresses. The play's setting is Málaga, during the filming of a movie. Except for Carbajosa, a reporter for a Madrid magazine, the characters are all members of the production company. The play's central incident is the death of Mary Cruz, the principal actress of the film production. She has recently died when the play begins: her funeral is represented in the prologue and epilogue, which occur chronologically before the main body of action. The play's seven central scenes take place after Mary's death and concern themselves with discovering its circumstances and causes. Thus, *The Banquet,* like *Nocturnal Assault* and *Death Thrust,* is essentially a long investigation of an unhappy event. The play's denouement is revealed in the prologue; suspense is thus eliminated from the outset and the dramatist can concentrate on sifting through the many factors—real and apparent, immediate and remote—that led to Mary's death. In so doing he develops the themes of exploitation and anthropophagy and suggests a general conclusion to be drawn from the findings of the investigation.

The circumstances of Mary's death gradually come into focus through a persistent probing, carried out in carefully planned dialogues and given form via the dramatic devices discussed above. The picture that emerges is not a pretty one. Mary committed suicide after being raped during the filming of an erotic scene in a pornographic movie. She was the victim of the uncontrolled desires of the actor with whom she was making the scene, but more fundamentally her violation and death were due to a vicious system of exploitation, cunningly conceived and executed by the director, Antonelli. Mary had been contracted to act in a ridiculous but arousing bit of erotica entitled "La carne humana" ("Human Flesh"). Aware that the film was artistically worthless, and that it would require her to participate in some suggestive scenes, she had nevertheless accepted the role, for two reasons: she was a young, unknown actress in need of "exposure," and she needed money with which to live until becoming an established actress. What Mary had not known was that Antonelli actually intended to make two versions of the film: one for local consumption, acceptable to Spanish censors, and another, more violent and more lascivious, for distribution outside Spain. Thus, in filming "Human Flesh," Antonelli had employed a frequent trick: in preparing for the erotic scenes, he had instructed the actor, Paco Rodas, to take more physical liberties with the actress than those originally rehearsed and agreed upon. Unfortunately, Rodas was somewhat intoxicated when the rape scene was to be filmed. The provocative nature of the situation caused him to lose self-control, and as the scene grew in intensity, so did his passions, until the fictitious rape became reality.

The play's moral statement involves a strong attack on the commercial film industry, which has turned art into an article of mass consumption and made the acting profession a source of alienation comparable to any other form of work in a modern industrial society. The film has become a capitalist enterprise which can function only by using its workers, ignoring their personal needs, and obliging them to perform functions that leave them frustrated and degraded. The film of an industrialized age has nothing to do with art, and its actors suffer the same personality split characteristic of all workers in a capitalist society. In the cinema, as in other industries, economic necessity and emphasis on competition mean that the work chooses the worker, rather than vice versa. Actors become, to a greater or lesser degree, the slaves of the producers, just as a factory worker is the slave of the capitalist for whom he works. The plot of *The Banquet* concerns the fate of one particular actress, but the incidental observations of the characters (especially during the long round-table discussion in Scene iv) make it clear that the case of Mary Cruz contains some general truths concerning art, capitalism, and human dignity.

The Fantastic Tavern differs slightly from the other epic plays, in that it takes place entirely in one location (a tavern in a working-class neighborhood of Madrid), and its plot is relatively uncomplicated. In other respects, however, *The Fantastic Tavern* features the formal details characteristic of the epic theater. It is a long, rambling drama of the *quinquilleros*—a numerous group which, like the Gypsies, lives outside the mainstream of Spanish society. There is no exact English translation of *quinquillero*. A *quinquillero* is roughly the equivalent of a tinker with regard to the work he performs, but in Spanish the word has a social, as well as occupational, connotation. In his preface to *The Fantastic Tavern* Sastre explains the trade of the *quinquilleros* and their social alienation, to which he has attempted to give dramatic form:

The principal characters of *The Fantastic Tavern* belong to a world which recently has made frequent news in the Spanish press: the world of the *quinquilleros*. The trade of these people is nomadic. They have no ethnic peculiarity, but they are a socially marginal group, having always been frustrated in their attempts at social integration. Wherever he lives, the *quinquillero* is "'The Other."

. . . .

In spite of their nomadic tradition, the *quinquilleros* are becoming increasingly located around fixed places of residence, almost always wretched, on the fringes of the cities. They live in caves, tents, lean-tos, and lately in "housing projects." . . . The *quinquilleros* have traditionally been wandering houseware merchants; now they specialize in repairing kitchen utensils, umbrellas, chairs, plumbing fixtures, milk jugs, etc.

The miserable conditions in which they live—social abandonment, cultural vacuum—create in these people a private morality, language, and life style. Naturally, these conditions constitute a breeding ground for petty delinquency, which undoubtedly exists among the *quinquilleros* in greater proportion than among other groups in society. But a *quinquillero* is not automatically a delinquent and bands of *quinquilleros* are not criminal gangs, contrary to the uninformed or maliciously distorted assertions of much of the Spanish press in its coverage of some recent episodes. By presenting the *quinquilleros* in a bad light, of course, the press merely intensifies their social entrapment and thus encourages a greater defensive delinquency on their part.[3]

The plot and moral statement of *The Fantastic Tavern* are essentially an illustration of the social and personal circumstances of the *quinquilleros*, as outlined in Sastre's introductory note. Rogelio, a *quinquillero*, returns to his neighborhood and goes to the Gato Negro tavern—a local gathering place and the setting for the entire play. He is wanted by the police because of some petty crime, and he has dared to return home only because his mother has just died and he wishes to attend her burial. During the course of the play Rogelio wanders in and out of the tavern, becoming increasingly intoxicated, having varied encounters with others who come in, and forgetting to go to his mother's burial. Near the end of the play he is fatally stabbed by an old enemy who then, in turn, becomes a fugitive from the police. The perspective in which Sastre places the events of the play makes it clear that he views the *quinquilleros* as an oppressed, alienated group whose social offenses and personal crudeness are to be blamed on the society that has excluded them.

III *Historical Epic Plays*

In *Roman Chronicles* and *The Blood and the Ashes* Sastre uses an historical setting in his attempt to find an effective revolutionary theater based on epic principles. *Roman Chronicles* relates the story of Numantia, a Spanish city to which Roman invaders laid siege in the year 153 B.C. After an heroic resistance of twenty years, seeing that a Roman victory was near, the citizens of Numantia burned their city and committed mass suicide, rather than let themselves become prisoners of the Romans. The saga of Numantia has been immortalized in Cervantes' drama *El cerco de Numancia* (*The Siege of Numantia*). Sastre's treatment of the story is designed to illuminate parallels between ancient Roman imperialism and modern imperialism of other nations—principally that of the United States in Vietnam. The play's twenty-six scenes are thus sprinkled with contemporary allusions proper to an anti-militarist, anti-imperialist ideology.

Roman Chronicles is the fourth of the series of plays which begins in 1965 with *The Blood and the Ashes*—the fourth of the works which Sastre terms "complex tragedies." In the preface Sastre makes explicit the experimental, anti-commercial nature of this and other works of the epic series: "This play has been written decidedly *outside* the professional and mercantile system of the Spanish theater."[4] Sastre dedicates the play to Spain's university theater groups, in the hope that this and other pieces for a contemporary revolutionary theater will stimulate a renewed energy in the university theaters.

Roman Chronicles is a successful piece of work, with reference to Sastre's declared aim of surpassing Brecht in search of a powerful theater of revolution. The play is extremely long and at times a bit tedious, but Sastre's intent, as explicitly stated in the prologue, was to offer many related scenes which could be effectively performed individually or in different combinations. And some of the scenes are indeed effective. In the best moments of *Roman Chronicles* Sastre has extracted from his dramatic situation a theatrical power that was always latent in the Brechtian form, but was seldom exploited by the great German dramatist, who was more concerned with propaganda than with the theatrical representation of a radical consciousness. Of the major contemporary dramatists, only Peter Weiss, in his monumental *Marat/Sade,* has fully exploited the devastating shock potential of the epic form in a manner comparable to Sastre's achievements. *Roman Chronicles* does, in fact, frequently make one think of *Marat/Sade.* Scene xxii is characterized by a grim black humor, produced by the citizens' exaggerated courtesy in helping each other die before the Romans enter the city. The following scene is introduced by this stage setting: "As the light returns, dawn is breaking and corpses are piled all over the stage, in every possible place and every possible position. Countless objects, including furniture, form a huge, shapeless mountain. Pieces of clothing are strewn about like scarecrows. All is burning, as a great bonfire" (p. 69). As the Romans march victoriously into the city, they find "the plaza filled with corpses and hanging manikins. The bonfire still smoulders. A film of black and grey ash covers everything. There is a terrible silence" (p. 72).

In the play's final scene there is a total fusion of fiction and reality. As a Roman soldier is about to destroy the flag of the occupied city, a student comes from the audience onto the stage. He asks the actor not to destroy the flag and announces to the audience that students have decided to occupy the theater and use it for revolutionary cultural events. More students climb onto the stage, one of them bringing the news that police have surrounded the theater. Another announces that Alfonso Sastre has been arrested in the lobby, charged with instigating the disturbances. A student begins to recite a revolutionary poem. He is interrupted by cries from the audience: a gentleman has suffered a heart attack, the police are entering the theater. As the tension and confusion reach maximum intensity, one of the "students" laughingly breaks the mood and tells the audience:

> Here end our *Roman Chronicles,* while in a thousand places the struggle goes on. Oh, incidentally, don't be surprised if you really do run into the police on your way out. Just in case, it might be a good idea to have your identification ready. Good night—and good luck. (*Curtain. At the exit, assuming the police are not actually there, some actors dressed as policemen will ask to see the identification of the more suspicious spectators.*) (p. 77)

The epic play in which Sastre reaches his highest peak of excellence, however, is not *Roman Chronicles* but *The Blood and the Ashes.* The earliest and finest example of Sastre's new revolutionary theater, this is the play in which Brecht's legacy is most fruitfully blended with a modern radical consciousness, the dialectic of history envisioned with greatest maturity, the tragedy of the individual reformer captured with sharpest sensitivity. The tempting comparisons with Brecht and Weiss, inevitably suggested by Sastre's epic phase, must be formulated above all with regard to *The Blood and the Ashes.*

The subtitle of *The Blood and the Ashes*—"Dialogues of Miguel Servet"—is a reference to the play's central character: a Spanish physician and theologian who, in 1553, fell victim to Calvinist fanaticism and was burned at the stake in Geneva.[5] The play is characterized by the episodic structure and alienation devices typical of the epic theater. It is a long work; although it has never been performed, its playing time would appear to be at least four hours. The plot of this biographical drama is set against the tumultuous background of the Reformation. It consists essentially of the difficulties that befall Miguel Servet as he attempts to deflate established notions about the circulation of the blood and to publicize his heretical unitarian theology. Servet is persecuted by the Inquisition and imprisoned in Vienne, France. He escapes and eventually ends up in Geneva, where he is again captured and finally put to death. Two bitter enemies—the Calvinists and the Catholics—collaborate to eliminate this reformer whose extraordinary mind had posed a threat to both of them.

Typically of the non-Aristotelian drama, however, the most gripping feature of *The Blood and the Ashes* is not its plot. Sastre's major accomplishment here is not his "arrangement of the incidents," but rather the character he has created in Miguel Servet, and the revolutionary ideology implicit in this character. In Servet Sastre has created the kind of character he had attempted, with far less success, in his William Tell a decade earlier. Sastre's Servet is an effective example of the demythified hero: the "human" hero, the giant of history who has been encrusted and distorted by legend and is now again reduced to human proportions, in order that his genius be recognizable in human terms and inspirational to contemporary human endeavors. The protagonist of *The Blood and the Ashes* lies, fears death, wavers in his convictions, is sexually impotent, and has bowel movements. He is the antithesis of the mythic hero but the epitome of the superior man. His vision offers humanity an expanded understanding of itself, and Sastre's characterization implies that this vision can be more convincingly transmitted by a fellow human than by an idealized caricature of a man.

The work which immediately suggests itself for comparison is Brecht's *The Life of Galileo.* Both Galileo and Servet were Renaissance men of science whose research and discoveries threatened an established order which happened to be under the vigilance of ecclesiastical authorities. Both men were persecuted by these authorities, who saw that the bases of their power would be undermined by a new way of viewing the world. Brecht's Galileo, like Sastre's Servet, is riddled with human frailties. Sastre's protagonist falsely denies authorship of incriminating treatises and becomes hysterical upon hearing his death sentence; Brecht's Galileo falsely claims credit for invention of the telescope and recants his teachings before the Inquisition, murmuring "Unhappy the land that is in need of heroes."[6]

A more fundamental point of contact between the two works lies in their profoundly revolutionary meaning, projected through imagery and ideas as well as through characterization. The real conflict in both these works is between courage and fear, enlightenment and obscurantism, innovation and rigidity, mobility and paralysis, flexibility and absolutism. This eternal dialectic is no less essential to contemporary struggles for social change than to an earlier resistance to theological tyranny. The two are analogues, and the perceptive spectator will see his own world suggested in the structure of past conflicts without the dubious help of explicit, dramatically debilitating propaganda.

Brecht's own notes make clear the analogy intended in *The Life of Galileo*: "Casting the Church as an embodiment of authority in this theatrical trial of the persecutors of the champions of free research does not help to secure an acquittal for the Church. But it would be highly dangerous, particularly nowadays, to treat a matter like Galileo's fight for freedom of research as a religious one; for thereby attention would be most unhappily deflected from present-day reactionary authorities of a totally unecclesiastical kind."[7] In the play itself there is a fundamental suggestion that men resist analysis and verification, preferring instead to base their lives on a system of myths which presents the world as a structure carefully ordered by absolute truths that need no verification. Belief in that structure is not based on any personal observation, but on the dictates of an Authority, accepted as omniscient in order to simplify the task of maintaining order. Nowhere in the play is this absolutist world view more forcefully exemplified than in Scene iv. A traditionalist philosopher admonishes Galileo: "The cosmos of the divine Aristotle, with its mystical, music-making spheres and crystal domes and the gyrations of its heavenly bodies and the oblique angle of the sun's orbit and the secrets of the satellite tables and the rich catalogue of constellations in the southern hemisphere and the inspired construction of the celestial globe, is a concept of such symmetry and beauty that we should do well to hesitate before disturbing that harmony."[8] This astronomical imagery permeates the play and defines the conflicting world views. Galileo believes that the heavens are open and free; his adversaries maintain that they are compartmentalized by crystal spheres. Galileo's telescope has shown him that the earth revolves and rotates; the traditionalists know only an earth that is static. The imagery evoked by these points of contention clarifies Galileo's efforts on behalf of philosophical freedom and mobility: efforts opposed, in this case, by the Catholic Church, but in principle abhorrent to any authority and to the mass of men who need authority.

Like *The Life of Galileo, The Blood and the Ashes* rests on the underlying assumption that to fight for truth—at any level—is to fight for human dignity. This is the revolutionary sense of the play's epigraph, taken from the epilogue: "Let's leave things as they should be—*not as they were.*"[9] This is, in fact, precisely the proposition to which Miguel Servet dedicates his life. The obscurantism that litters his path is not only intellectually offensive, but is a concrete source of material misery and injustice. His struggle to clarify the thinking of men necessarily implies a revised social order, because it would lead to new modes of human relations. This fact is made especially clear in an early scene in which Servet questions the value of bloodletting as a medical treatment. An elderly physician replies that Servet's methods are "strange and revolutionary" because they are too gentle to cure the patient's "punished body." Servet's defense of his methods links theological ideas to medical theories and clarifies the humanistic value of truth:

Illness is not a punishment of the body, as you have said. That is an erroneous notion, thoughtlessly carried over from theology. It implies that the patient is guilty of something of which he knows nothing, and that God sends the illness as a punishment. We still believe that a sick man has in his body demons that must be driven out in the bloodiest possible way. We still flagellate madmen and lock them in dark dungeons, where they are subjected to mistreatment and humiliation. This is to say nothing of the murderous bloodlettings so frequently performed on the ill. I would have you know, sir, that patients should be bled only when they have an excess of blood. Medicine should be kind. (pp. 15-16)

Religious persecution of the Anabaptists, the sect to which Servet belongs, is social persecution as well: "We are persecuted, Miguel, for theological reasons, but more than anything because we advocate libertarian communism. The rich and the royal see us as sinners in the frightful image of the Antichrist! Distribution of the wealth! For them, that *is* the Antichrist, and they defend their perverse idea with oppressive force!" (p. 23). The epitome of oppressive theocracy, John Calvin, is significantly opposed to scientific discovery, because it poses a threat to the order from which his power derives:

I should like to advise Your Honors the Magistrates of the wisdom of curtailing this sort of "scientific" idiocy that threatens the spiritual integrity of our communty. You will recall the notion that was published ten years ago under the title 'De Revolutionibus Orbium Caelestium' and has been secretly circulating ever since. As though we were not clearly told, in Psalm 93, verse 1, that "the world is established, that it cannot be moved." Does there live the man who would dare to place the authority of that so-called monk, Copernicus, above the word of the Holy Spirit? Sirs, I tell you such monsters should be suffocated! (pp. 110-11)

While attending to victims of the plague at a hospital in Vienne, Miguel is informed that human actions, motivated by fear and superstition, have expanded the effects of a natural calamity. "Many of the people you see here—in fact, the majority—are Jews who were in good health when they came, and are now as wretched as the rest of us. They were locked up here because they were accused of poisoning the water and sticking the Devil's excrement on the doors of many good Christian homes. Two of them—a father and his four-year-old son—were lynched for that very reason the other day in the meat market" (pp. 43-44).

The Blood and the Ashes offers a unified vision of truth, freedom, and dignity. The play is conceived and constructed on

the premise that the three are inseparable. Its revolutionary statement is powerful because of this rich variety of perspective from which it is offered. It is not formulated with regard to a particular contemporary cause, but rather in terms of the fundamental, timeless dialectic of social change: the forces of stagnation confronted by the forces of mobility. The fact that Servet's demise is due to the ironic collaboration of Catholics and Calvinists strongly suggests that his "heresy" was not so much a threat to a particular doctrine as to monolithic authoritarian structures in general, all of which are essentially oppressive. The epilogue is a vivid representation of this dialectic and a summary of the play's revolutionary ideology. The curtain rises on a bare pedestal which, in the prologue, had held a bust of Miguel Servet. The bust was quickly smashed by Nazi soldiers and the pedestal later became Servet's execution platform. Sebastián, a minor character turned narrator, addresses the audience:

And now the pedestal stands bare,
and there rises up in us
the memory of a man who was of flesh and blood,
now reduced to ash.
The point, my friends, is to build a new world
—(We don't need statues)—
where blood does not flow and the ground is not strewn with the ashes of those who were whole men, true men,
—(Why so many statues?)—
a world where we can study and work
—(Smash the statues!)—
a world where men can live
and socialism prosper.
The play has ended. Good night. (pp. 151-52)

IV *Significance of the Epic Phase*

In reflecting upon the significance of Sastre's epic theater in the context of his total production, one thinks immediately of Sastre's analysis of the twentieth-century theater, first published in 1963 and reprinted in *Anatomy of Realism*. Modifying his earlier notion that the serious contemporary theater represented a linear evolution of Naturalism, Sastre wrote: "I find in the present-day theater of the Western world three tendencies: *three and only three* . . .: the epic, the dramatic, and the van-

guard. These tendencies represent . . . three distinct negations of Naturalism" (*AR*, 215). Although different in their image of man and in details of form, the three shared a common ground which, Sastre predicted, would allow them eventually to fuse into a new theater—a synthesis of the varied experiences of the dramatic art in the twentieth century.

With his epic theater Sastre has now explored all three of these tendencies and has made progress toward the new theater of synthesis. He has passed from early avant-garde experiments to a theater of social realism based on Aristotelian principles, and ultimately to his post-Brechtian theater characterized by alienation devices. This evolution is a further indication of the conceptual link between Sastre's critical and creative work.

It is essential to understand that Sastre's newest direction does not represent a reversal in his thought and dramaturgy, but is simply the latest step of the dialectical evolution characteristic of his work since 1950. Insofar as Sastre's epic phase involves a return to the non-Aristotelian theater of an earlier period, the three major directions of his theater may be abstractly visualized as three stages of a dialectical process: action-reaction-renewal. However, one must consider that each new stage of a dialectic brings with it an expanded awareness born of synthesized previous experiences. No new stage of development ever represents a total break with the past or a complete return to the starting point. In his epic plays Sastre has not negated his previous work, but rather enlarged upon it, just as he has enlarged upon his model (Brecht) by exploiting the radical aesthetic of alienation devices more thoroughly than Brecht ever did.

Antecedents to Sastre's epic phase are found in abundance in his earlier work. *Nocturnal Assault* is an early, tentative exploration of the epic form. *Office of Darkness,* although not epic in form, features a slangy, whimsical dialogue that sets it apart from the other dramas of social realism and relates it to the epic plays. *Sad Are the Eyes of William Tell* is characterized by dark humor and a demythified hero; one or both of these devices are present in *Roman Chronicles, The Fantastic Tavern,* and *The Blood and the Ashes.* With regard to dramatic form, the epic plays have antecedents in both of Sastre's earlier periods. In their use of narrative elements, their non-psychological characterization, and their problematic unity, they are related to

the dramas of frustration. In the use of flashbacks, prologue and epilogue, and numerous *cuadros* in place of three acts, the epic plays are antedated by several dramas of social realism. *Pathetic Prologue, The Condemned Squad, The Gag, The Red Earth, Death in the Neighborhood,* and *Sad Are the Eyes of William Tell,* although founded on basic Aristotelian principles of empathy and unity of plot, all have this fluid, mobile construction. Even *In the Net,* Sastre's tensest and most tightly unified drama, contains two details more proper to the epic theater than to the dramatic: the final word of dialogue is directed to the audience, and the acts bear titles. These elements are actually somewhat out of place here, given the play's dramatic situation and its construction, but their presence betokens Sastre's long, latent affinity for the epic form.

Sastre's epic theater thus represents evolution and synthesis, rather than reversal and total negation. It has come about through its author's ever expanding awareness of the meaning of revolution and of its proper aesthetic translation. The previously used forms and techniques which recur in the epic plays are used there in ways that reflect this expanded consciousness. The non-Aristotelian forms of the dramas of frustration are now used in function of a revolutionary ideology. The fragmented construction of some dramas of social realism is now intensified and combined with other alienation devices, in consequence of Sastre's sharpened perception of the ideological assumptions implicit in the Aristotelian call for unity, logic, and purgation. Sastre had always wanted to "go beyond" catharsis, even when he was writing Aristotelian drama; he had wanted the theater to be more than an emotional laxative. He had long been aware of modern man's schizoid condition and had attempted to reflect it in his dramas, as a first step toward overcoming it. He had seen theater as investigation and agitation—as a means of helping humanity to see through the immobilizing myths that confound man's understanding of his world—and he had been aware that naturalism posed a formidable obstacle to this objective by lending respectability to a familiar, but unacceptable, world order.

In short, the epic theater was the only logical place for Sastre to go after social realism, given his persistent self-examination and self-renewal, his insistence on a multiple perspective, and his radical consciousness. His long, complicated

dialectical process has brought him to a profound vision of revolution, and to an art form appropriate to that vision. If producers or audiences react negatively, as well they may, to *The Banquet, The Fantastic Tavern, Roman Chronicles,* and *The Blood and the Ashes,* their reaction will confirm the epic theater's fundamental assumption: that the essential first step of revolution is to persuade men that the world they see around them is not the only world possible, to encourage them to tolerate unfamiliar images of themselves, and to break down the mental rigidity fostered by the myths of an unjust society.

CHAPTER 8

Sastre's Prose Works

I Red Flowers for Miguel Servet

ALTHOUGH Sastre's literary importance is unquestionably due to his dramatic and critical writings, he is also the author of three prose works that require mention. In June, 1964, Sastre took time out from his work on *The Blood and the Ashes* to begin a short literary biography of the protagonist of that play. Five months later this work was completed and bore the title *Flores rojas para Miguel Servet* (*Red Flowers for Miguel Servet*). Although it is self-contained, this biography can profitably be read as a companion to *The Blood and the Ashes.* It is not intended as an explanation of Sastre's epic play; indeed, the only mention of the play in *Red Flowers* occurs in the prologue. But a consecutive reading of the two works heightens the reader's appreciation of both of them. Their forms are radically different, one being an episodic work for the theater, the other a biographical narrative. Each brings its own style and perspective to the life and death of Servet. The two works are complementary treatments of the same subject; each enhances the power and clarity of the other.

As biography and history *Red Flowers* does not pretend to illuminate any previously unknown facts. Rather, it is simply a readable, compact account of Servet's life from birth to death. The circumstances of this martyr's fate emerge clearly from Sastre's pages, which include numerous documents, letters, and quotations from writings by and about Servet. The fact that this is a "literary" rather than scholarly biography does not mean that Sastre has approached history in a whimsical or impressionistic manner. His subject has been carefully researched, and its presentation is well supported with dates and details.

The philosophical and ideological statements of *Red Flowers* are essentially those noted in *The Blood and the Ashes.* The constant of Servet's varied and turbulent life is presented as his passionate search for unity in all reality. "For Servet," writes Sastre, "reality moves toward a universal unity."[1] His theology is unitarian and pantheistic. His God is one, not three, and He is embodied in all creation. He is described variously as an "omnifarious mind," "omnifarious essence," and "multimodal unity" (p. 124). Servet's God is, in short, the dialectical unity of reality. Likewise, Servet's discovery that blood and air mix in the lungs is due to his belief that the human body, like all creation, functions on principles of unity and synthesis. The violence, humiliation, and physical destruction to which Servet is subjected are especially ironic in that they are perpetrated against a man whose life had been a quest for unity and integrity, correlatives of human dignity. A man who was alive and whole is broken down into ashes, and even his ashes disperse as they are cast to the wind.

The forces that defeat Servet's quest for wholeness are, by definition, enemies of human dignity and agents of oppression. As in *The Blood and the Ashes,* a social ideology is cast in terms of a basic dialectic between the humanitarian conscience and the forces of human degradation. In this case the former is embodied in Servet's own thought and in the dawning democratic spirit of sixteenth-century Europe; the latter is personified by John Calvin, whose theocratic rule has turned Geneva into a police state and who is personally responsible for Servet's death. Sastre's presentation makes clear that Servet's religious persecution is essentially social oppression: he is arrested, tried, and executed in clear violation of his civil rights and the norms of due process. As in *The Blood and the Ashes,* there is a suggestion that truth, personal integrity, and social justice are interrelated aspects of a general struggle for human liberation.

The literary effectiveness of this biography resides primarily in Sastre's carefully controlled, deliberately archaic style, and the subtle echo of Don Quixote that pervades the book. These qualities suggest another comparison with *The Blood and the Ashes,* for there, too, one notes a carefully guarded style in the dialogue, as well as some subtle, almost subliminal associations between Servet and Don Quixote. But in Sastre's epic play these associations are complicated by the epic form and theatrical genre of the work. In *Red Flowers* the medium is only the printed word and Sastre can be much more thorough in his warm parody of Cervantes' masterpiece.

There is, of course, an obvious philosophic affinity between Miguel Servet and Don Quixote, in the quest for absolute, uncontradictory truth that defines both their lives. In addition, Sastre employs two major literary devices to evoke the shadows of Don Quixote that dart in and out of his portrait of Miguel Servet: his presentation of the quixotic personality and experience of Servet, and details of the book's form and style. With tongue in cheek Sastre explains that Servet evolved his heretical ideas after he had been exposed to certain books which "were to confound his senses" (p. 32). Servet, "like the Knight of the Mournful Countenance, passed his nights from dusk to dawn, and his days from dawn to dusk, reading those books . . ." (p. 33). Sastre imagines a squire, named Benito, who accompanied Servet for several years in his wanderings: "When the two left to return home, theirs was a strange appearance in the lonely streets at twilight. As they passed by the windows from which timid eyes stared, they offered an unreal scene set against a heavy silence: Miguel, tall and sad on his horse, and Benito, deep in thought on his dark colored donkey" (p. 138). In speculating on Servet's mysterious reason for taking his fatal journey to Geneva, Sastre suggests that it was merely a further stage of Servet's quixotic, absolutist quest: "Was Miguel unconsciously choosing his destiny? Was he guilty of an unconscious bad faith in choosing entrapment as a form of liberation and salvation? Even admitting that he was not deliberately seeking a confrontation with The Enemy, can we doubt that his quixotic heart really desired one?" (pp. 163-64).

In support of the philosophical and personal parallels between Servet and Don Quixote, Sastre has organized his book in a markedly Cervantine manner. He begins it with quotations from Marcelino Menéndez y Pelayo, Stefan Zweig, and Antonio Machado which call attention to physical and spiritual resemblances between Servet and Don Quixote. There follows a section modeled after the beginning of *Don Quixote*: a collection of assorted epigrams and apocryphal poems in praise of Miguel Servet. Next, a prologue, written in the archaic style of the entire book, in which Sastre gives a brief portrait of Servet, stressing possible points of contact between him and Don Quixote. Finally, the book's two parts and forty-three chapters bear long, analytical titles, just as do those of Cervantes' masterpiece: "Wherein Are Related His General Medical Ideas, with

Respect to a Work Handed Over to the Printer Shortly Before the Events Recorded in the Previous Chapter" (Part I, Ch. 9); or "Which Informs of Events in Vienne Following Miguel's Flight, and of the Grief that Would Have Befallen Him Had He not Fled" (I, 25). These persistent yet subtle evocations of Cervantes' immortal hero bring an attention-compelling tone and perspective to Sastre's treatment of Miguel Servet and contribute to the delightfully entertaining quality of this book.

II El paralelo 38 (The 38th Parallel)

Sastre's only novel is a short, moderately interesting work written in 1958 and published in 1965 after minor revisions.[2] Its action begins and ends at a roadside café, the name of which constitutes the novel's title. The major source of tension and action is the antagonism between two truck drivers who habitually stop at the café: Luis, frail and nervous, and Pedro el Gordo, a massive, boisterous bully. After much unprovoked harassment, Pedro challenges Luis to a game of "Chicken" on the highway: the two drivers will drive down the highway in opposite directions, turn around, and drive back toward each other at a high speed, meeting in front of the "Paralelo." The object of the game is to see which of the drivers loses his nerve first and leaves the road. True to Pedro's prediction, Luis loses and is humiliated. Both drivers then continue their journeys, Pedro to the coast and Luis to Madrid.

Upon arriving at his home in Madrid, Luis discovers that his unstable domestic situation has grown worse during his absence. His young, discontented wife has taken to the streets in search of amusement, leaving their child alone in the apartment. After an extended search Luis finds her in a nightclub, in the arms of a young lover. In a fit of rage Luis attacks his wife and her companion; he is restrained by onlookers and ejected from the nightclub. The following morning he places a long distance telephone call to the "Paralelo" to announce that he will be there with his truck at noon, and that this time he does not intend to clear the road for Pedro. Word of the impending showdown quickly spreads; a large crowd gathers to watch as the two trucks collide in front of the café. Both drivers are killed instantly. Several days later a stranger, who had wandered into the "Paralelo" just before the fatal crash, returns and chats at length with the owners and customers, informing himself of the antecedents and circumstances of the catastrophe. The stranger proves to be the "author" of the story.

Although not a major literary accomplishment, *The 38th Parallel* poses some interesting relationships to the rest of Sastre's work. That is, the intrinsic literary value of this novel is not outstanding, but it contains elements that clarify or reinforce tendencies visible in Sastre's work as a whole. Perhaps the most interesting of these is Sastre's desire—expressed in the prologue and manifest in the novel—to explore ways of overcoming barriers among artistic genres. A search for common ground among the genres had been a frequent subject of Sastre's essays starting around 1955 and had been one basis for Sastre's admiration of Brecht: he regarded the German dramatist as the writer who had liberated the theater from "the old restraints of formal rigidity and strict separation of genres."[3] Furthermore, in addition to his dramatic and critical writings, Sastre had long evidenced an interest in the cinema. Some of his early essays, written prior to *Drama and Society,* had been film reviews. One essay in *Anatomy of Realism* deals with Michelangelo Antonioni. Sastre is the author of seven screenplays: "Amanecer en puerta oscura" ("Dawn Through a Dark Door"), 1956, "Tres hombres" ("Three Men"), 1957, "Carmen" (1958), "La noche y el alba' ("The Night and the Dawn"), 1957, "Un hecho violento" ("A Violent Affair"), 1957, "A las cinco de la tarde" ("At Five in the Afternoon"), 1960,[4] and "Nunca pasa nada" ("Nothing Ever Happens"), 1961. Of these titles, the last four became films. The use of cinematic techniques in the epic plays and *Anna Kleiber,* and the subject matter of *The Banquet,* are further indications of Sastre's interest in the artistic potential of the cinema.

In the prologue to *The 38th Parallel* Sastre affirms that "the genres are not isolated from each other; on the contrary, points of contact among the genres are not only possible, but frequent . . ."[5] Specifically, the generic characteristics of this novel are those of narrative prose, drama, and screen play. This hybrid derives from Sastre's interest in "the problem of the so-called 'screen play' as literature."[6] *The 38th Parallel* is essentially an expanded screen play—a skeletal plot onto which a certain amount of narrative padding has been added for the sake of a more readable text. The cinematic conception of the work accounts for a high degree of mobility, a frequently changing perspective which corresponds to the effect of a roving camera. This technique is especially effective as the two truck drivers go their separate ways and then hurtle back toward each other with deadly intent. As the distance between them grows shorter, the narrative moves back and forth from one driver to the other with increasing speed, thus creating an impression similar to that of a film sequence composed of rapidly alternating perspectives.

Given this cinematic conception and technique, it is not surprising to find a highly dramatic quality in the structure of the novel's conflict. The method and terminology of dramatic analysis would render the following picture of the novel:

ACT I (Exposition and Point of Attack): The novel's beginning, through the first game of "Chicken."

ACT II (Complication and Turning Point): Luis's arrival in Madrid, through his telephone call to the "Paralelo."

ACT III (Denouement): Luis's drive back to the "Paralelo" and the fatal crash.

EPILOGUE: The events that follow the crash: the return of the "stranger" and his conversations with people at the "Paralelo."

Except for the brief "epilogue," the entire novel moves toward the climactic fatal crash. Adversaries are clearly defined and developed; tension is maintained throughout. Well over half the novel's text is dialogue, and the narrative material has the sketchy quality of stage directions.

The 38th Parallel contains several other points of contact with Sastre's other work. There is a brief reference to the *quinquilleros* (p. 14)—an indication of Sastre's sensitivity to the problems of the social group later to be treated in detail in *The Fantastic Tavern*. The novel's dialogue is the rough, vulgar speech of the working class, as is the dialogue of *The Fantastic Tavern*. *The 38th Parallel* contains a distantiation device found in several of Sastre's plays: the appearance of the "author" as a character. Sastre makes this touch especially effective by withholding the stranger's identity until the last line of the novel. With this surprising last-minute revelation, the events of the novel suddenly appear in a radically altered light. The presence of the author in his own novel constitutes an extra "layer" in the aesthetic experience; it pushes the reader back from the literary object, thus causing the latter to appear not as a copy of objective reality, but as a shocking transformation of it.

Ideologically, *The 38th Parallel* is related to the rest of Sastre's work in its image of a divided humanity, represented structurally in the antagonism between Luis and Pedro. The games of "Chicken" are microcosms of an unhealthy society: the antagonists are either polarized or colliding in fatal encounter, while the spectators, helpless to prevent the slaughter, look on with curiosity, horror, or apathy. The café's unusual name calls attention to its function as a point of demarcation and deadly encounter. The ideological intent of *The 38th Parallel* is summarized in Sastre's introductory verse:

O Simple Tale
of Painful Deeds, Grief and Suicide.
Cry Against Brutality
and Protest of Man's Abandonment.
May We Someday See the Oneness
Of Those Who Are Today Asunder. (p. 5)

III Las noches lúgubres (Lugubrious Nights)

The dark, brooding side of Sastre's mind returns to prominence in this collection of prose pieces written between 1961 and 1963. At once the most terrifying and most humorous of Sastre's works, *Lugubrious Nights* is also his most effective articulation of the anguish that lies at the heart of the existentialist vision. The book's three sections are permeated with various expressions of this anguish: an awareness of the gratuity and fragility of human existence and human order, a sense of the world's hostility toward the individual, a vague terror that springs from no concrete source but yet is a prime determinant of human behavior:

> It is not a question . . . of terror experienced in the face of an immediate, visible threat. We are not concerned here with terror produced by real pistols aimed at us, or by hooded executioners who stare at us, or by the gestures of the torturer who threatens to tighten the pincers around our ankles. The terror in these stories is of a different sort. It is the terror caused by invisible threats, real and unreal: vague threats that produce uncertainty, ambiguity, and disturbing confusion. The fact that the threat is invisible frequently makes its reality problematical, even if the menace in question is death itself.[7]

The tales of *Lugubrious Nights* are thus situated neither in a realm of total fantasy, nor of understandable, acceptable reality, but rather in the twilight zone of consciousness, where perceptions are clear enough to permit recognition of the world, but too vague to permit an ordering of that which is perceived. The result is a murky vision of a world in which order has either disappeared entirely or become an ironic agent of torment for disoriented human beings. Occasionally there is a "reason" or logical explanation for this breakdown of rational structure: alcoholism, delirium, mental illness, brainwashing. But the explanations are always relative and never totally satisfactory. Some measure of the disturbing experiences presented in these stories must always be attributed to causes beyond the grasp of the human mind.

The book's subject matter is well selected to enhance this ambiguous perception of reality, in that it consists of recognizable human experiences presented in an unfamiliar mode. Part I ("Nights of the Holy Spirit") is a tale of vampires in Madrid. Part II ("Delirium") is a nightmarish vision of the revival of Naziism. Port III ("The Cells of Terror") consists of twenty vignettes of terror and helplessness, the sources of which range from atomic holocaust to the hostile stare of strangers. In his preface Sastre writes of the "myths" which he has employed in an attempt to strike familiar but disturbing chords in his reader's consciousness: "an invisible presence, a premonition (usually of death), vampirism, metamorphosis, the return of the dead, the fabrication of a human being, the destruction of the world . . ." (p. 10).

Lugubrious Nights has antecedents in Sastre's dramatic literature. Its characteristic anguish suggests a clear affinity with all the dramas of frustration, its reliance on the unexplainable as a dramatic device is a repetition of the technique used in *The Raven,* and the black humor that rises so naturally from scenes of horror is a feature of several of Sastre's more mature plays. However, regardless of its affinities with Sastre's asocial dramas, *Lugubrious Nights* could be termed "literature of frustration" only in a very limited and relative sense. If one applies the fundamental critical criterion developed above—the distinction between an image of man's potentiality and an image of his helplessness—the stories of *Lugubrious Nights* clearly belong to the latter category. Unlike the dramas of frustration, however, *Lugubrious Nights* depicts human anguish not as a metaphysical affliction, but rather as a state of mind that has resulted from social madness—from man's failure to live with his fellows in a way that allows each individual to establish for himself a lucid, emotionally stable relationship with the world. The anxieties, neuroses, and hallucinations that compose the terror-ridden world of this book do not exist gratuituously. They exist because the characters are members of a human society that distorts the individual and his perceptions.

This social perspective of terror is implicit in the book's major themes, which Sastre sees as "some of the most fundamental bases of contemporary terror: alienation, the resurrection of Nazi-ism, social exploitation, witch hunts, police repression, nuclear war . . ." (p. 10). There are others: identity crisis, labyrinth, incommunication. These themes are elaborated in *Lugubrious Nights* in such a fashion as to illuminate the relation between individual teror and the awesome social realities with which a nervous world lives today. Unlike the less sophisticated dramas of frustration, *Lugubrious Nights* embodies a total vision of man—an interpretation of man's individual agonies as the reflection of his life in an evil society.

In this attempt to alter the reader's view of the world by handing him familiar material in a disturbing light, Sastre is seeking essentially the same psychological impact sought in his epic plays. It is thus not surprising to find in *Lugubrious Nights* some of the same distantiation techniques used in Sastre's most recent works for the theater. The most obvious of these techniques is the high degree of stylization with which the tales of *Lugubrious Nights* are presented. The narrative style has the contrived, archaic quality of nineteenth-century horror stories or serialized novels: sentences are long and complex, explanations are frequent and patronizing:

> By now I had returned to my bedroom, and while standing next to my bed I felt something grasp my left ankle; I emitted a scream and pulled back my foot, dragging, as I did so, a certain weight from under the bed; it was Isaiah, who had seized upon the aforesaid portion of my body with his two little hands (or with one of them: of this detail I cannot be certain); this was the motive for my screams (which the neighbors took for those of a dying man), and for my fruitless attempt to leave that location forthwith, and for the trampling which I imparted to the head of the hydrocephalic idiot, and for his horrible death. (p. 94)

Dialogues are equally stylized. Titles of stories and chapters are long and explanatory, analogous to the verbal or written announcements so frequently used at the beginning of acts or scenes in the epic theater. The author frequently abandons his narrative and addresses the reader directly, commenting on the story in progress—one of several forms of "literature within literature" employed in *Lugubrious Nights.* Fact and fantasy are skillfully blended until they can no longer be distinguished. The fantastic tale of vampires in Madrid, for example, is liberally punctuated with references to real, contemporary personages, places, and events: certain streets and areas of Madrid, Sastre's own address, Vicente Aleixandre, Manuel Fraga Iribarne.

Certain other details enhance this illusion of realism and consequently the labyrinthine entanglement of fantasy and fact: footnotes, sobriety of presentation, references to apocryphal documents on which the stories are supposedly based. These elements are agents of a disturbing illusion as well as a tongue-in-cheek humor which could well deceive an ingenuous reader. Perhaps the most humorous moment of the entire book is the final chapter of "Nights of the Holy Spirit"—a "requiem" for Arpad Vászary, the vampire who has finally died with a stake through his heart. This tribute to the slain vampire is an assortment of eight apocryphal published commentaries on his death, collected from the world's press and representing widely divergent sources and points of view. Each "commentator" interprets Vászary and the phenomenon of vampirism from the viewpoint of his own special interest; the tone of the comments ranges from hysterical paranoia to cold analysis, as vampirism becomes a ludicrous *cause célèbre.* The juxtaposition of differing tones and attitudes, and the serious presentation of absurd comments, produce an amusing picture of social idiocy. For example:

"Let us not deceive ourselves, friends. A. V. embodies the malignant spirit of our age. We must ever remain alert and on guard." (*Traditionalist Thought.* Pamplona: August, 1963.)

"A. V. was not the last of the vampires. Thousands more fly on and surround us in the night." (*The Interplanetarian: Magazine of Science, Magic and Progress.* Paris: November, 1963.)

"We feel compelled to point out that Vászary's murder was methodically planned in the laboratories of international Communism. His murderers are witting or unwitting puppets of Moscow. The order was given in Budapest by Janos Kadar, the Butcher of Hungary. Whether they are militants, fellow travelers, or merely useful fools, Vászary's murderers should be turned into an example. And this should be done regardless of the barking . . . of the Mason dogs and their paid agents, the Jews and Communists." (José Gómez, *Patriotic Christian Action,* n.d.)

"Du point de vue scientifique, il n'existe pas de vampyrs." (*Cahiers de Biologie.* Paris: October, p. 139.)[8]

How does this literature of fantasy, tongue-in-cheek humor, and contrived fictional devices relate to Sastre's revolutionary commitment? Why has Sastre attempted in this particular way to illuminate man's world and encourage its transformation? The answer to these questions is summarized in the concept of the "dialectical imagination," considered by Sastre in the book's preface. The illumination and transformation of human society depend on an expanded human consciousness, an increased capacity for mental images of human experience. Thus, in writing these stories Sastre has invoked a "free imagination," seeking to "determine the limit of the dialectical imagination" in himself and his readers. Sastre envisions the human imaginative faculty as a means to a dialectical, transcendent mode of viewing the world. The imagination permits a debate with the status quo, an opposition to stagnating myths. Western man, if he is to survive, must reactivate his imaginative faculties in order to transcend the oppressive structures that have crystallized around him in modern times: "I believe . . . that Western man . . . alienated and shrunken by a stifling socio-political structure, needs to recover his lost imagination at the highest possible level" (p. 11).

In other words, man's ability to imagine realities beyond those immediately available to him is a key to his ability to change his world. This capacity has been undermined by social and political institutions which thrive on mental lethargy. Mind-dazzling tricks, the terrifying collapse of daily reality, and disconcerting humor are some of the means by which Sastre attempts to liberate the human imagination in *Lugubrious Nights.* The unusual prose creations of this book represent yet another aspect of Sastre's long exploration of the interrelationships of art, psychology, and revolution. Like his dramas of penetrative realism and his epic plays, Sastre's prose writings suggest a dialectic, a tension between the everyday world and another world that is vaguely perceived. There arises from all this work a persistent, awesome suggestion that man's very survival may depend upon his ability to believe that, for better or for worse, that "other" world can become a reality.

CHAPTER 9

Conclusion

ULTIMATELY one sees in Alfonso Sastre's vision, and in its literary formulation, a desire to reintegrate modern man, alienated from himself, his fellow men, and the forces that control his life. A fundamental suggestion of Sastre's best work is that modern humanity is the fragmented, neurotic result of social systems that turn people into objects, foment a split between the individual's personal and social lives, and render the complete personality impossible. Recovery of this personal completeness is implicit in Sastre's call for a realism that reflects both extremes of the fragmented human being, with the hope of achieving synthesis, or reintegration. However, this recovery can be realized at the personal level only through the implantation of a humanistic social context for the individual's activities.

In his works for the theater and his prose writing Sastre uses the phenomenon of alienation as a dramatic element. It is the ultimate source of the loneliness and anguish that torment his characters. The acts through which his heroes find their authenticity are painful precisely because one can become a real human being (recover his humanity) only by establishing a burning friction between himself and the forces that undermine his integrity. The polarized forces that produce dramatic conflict in much of Sastre's work are precisely the individual and the vaguely perceived determinants of his destiny. The condemned squad suffers because its enemy is inscrutable, as do the characters of *The Raven*. Luis Opuls defines God as "absolutely different." The tyrant of William Tell's country is nicknamed "The Other" because he lives and thinks apart from the men whose lives he controls. Miguel Servet is consumed by a passion that drives him to seek unity in the universe. *Lugubrious Nights* presents imaginary human beings tormented by their inability to define the forces that pursue them. Until men become absolute ends, rather than objects, and until the individual knows, and becomes, the force that controls his life, unity will not be realized, and anguish will continue to be the prime characteristic of human existence.

Like the thinkers who have influenced him, Sastre realizes that man's existence can be meaningful only when he is free, and that freedom exists only as the correlative of fluidity, change, and ultimate reunification of the human being. The rational enunciation and aesthetic embodiment of these truths are the tasks to which Sastre has passionately dedicated himself.

Notes and References

Chapter One

1. Alfonso Sastre, *Drama y sociedad* (Madrid, 1956), p. 199.
2. Alfonso Sastre and José Mariá del Quinto, "Manifiesto del T.A.S.," in *Alfonso Sastre,* José Monleón, ed. (Madrid, 1964), pp. 99-102.
3. Further documents concerning the T.A.S. are found in Monleón's *Alfonso Sastre,* pp. 47-54, 83-88.
4. Alfonso Sastre and José María del Quinto, "Declaración del G.T.R.," *Primer acto,* 16 (Sept.-Oct., 1960), 45. Reprinted in *Alfonso Sastre,* pp. 117-18.
5. Documents concerning the G.T.R. are included in *Alfonso Sastre* and in Sastre's *Anatomía del realismo* (Barcelona, 1965).

Chapter Two

1. Personal interview with Quinto, March 24, 1965.
2. In Sastre's theater the religious crisis is evident in the plays written before *La mordaza* (1954) and it recurs sporadically in some works written later.
3. Alfonso Sastre, "La universidad y el teatro," *Guía* (May, 1951), p. 31.
4. Alfonso Sastre, "Contestación espontánea a una encuesta sobre teatro católico," *Correo literario,* 24 (May 15, 1951), 2.
5. Alfonso Sastre, "Del 'Teatro Católico,'" *Cuadernos hispanoamericanos,* 21 (May-June, 1951), 484.
6. Alfonso Sastre, "El teatro revolucionario," *Guía* (August, 1952), p. 22.
7. Alfonso Sastre, "Teología del drama," *Correo literario,* 85 (December 1, 1953), 10.
8. *Ibid.*
9. " 'Europa 1951', gran fracaso de Rosellini," *Cuadernos hispanoamericanos,* 48 (Dec., 1953), 331.
10. Alfonso Sastre, "Prólogo" to *Drama y sociedad* (Madrid, 1956), pp. 7-9.
11. Use of the *refrito*—i.e., repetition of a previously published article—has been a major device in Sastre's career as an essayist, not only in *Drama and Society* but in later works as well. In 1959, with

a tongue-in-cheek humor rare in his writings, Sastre offered a defense of this procedure: "In Spain people read so little, that if one wants something to be read, he must give the public several chances. I have the impression that an article published only once is, in effect, still unpublished. I would like to suggest that it is advisable to publish an item several times, in different magazines, varying the title in ways that will make the article appealing from any point of view. The benefit would be twofold: there would be the social contribution of a good article, as well as a personal benefit (that of the author, who would normally be in economic difficulties, because of the meager rewards which his efforts usually bring)." "El 'Refrito,'" *Informaciones* (May 2, 1959), p. 3.

12. "Prólogo," p. 9.

13. Ramón Barce, "'Drama y sociedad' por Alfonso Sastre," *Indice*, XII, 155 (August, 1958), 25. Other favorable comments on *Drama and Society* are found in José Julio Perlado, "En torno al teatro," *Nuestro Tiempo*, 29 (Nov., 1956), 46-48; and Pilar G. Suelto de Sáenz, "El teatro universitario español en los últimos treinta años," *Thesavrvs*, XIX, 3 (Sept.-Dec., 1964), 543-57.

14. Maeterlinck and Lenormand in Part II, Chapter 6, of *Drama y sociedad*, pp. 101-7; Lenormand and Maeterlinck in Part II, Chapter 17, of *Drama y sociedad*, pp. 153-56; Lenormand and O'Neill in "El teatro actual," *Revista española*, 5 (Jan.-Feb., 1954), 536-49; Lenormand in "Tragedia," *Correo literario*, 70 (April 15, 1953), 10, and "Documentos del teatro francés contemporáneo," *Cuadernos hispanoamericanos*, 31 (July, 1952), 158-59; Jardiel Poncela in "Un buen libro sobre el teatro español," *Cuadernos hispanoamericanos*, 49 (Jan., 1954), 127.

15. *Drama y sociedad*, pp. 202-3. Subsequent page references to *Drama and Society* will be included parenthetically in the text and will be indicated by the symbol *DS*.

16. "Muerte de dos dramaturgos," *Cuadernos hispanoamericanos*, 50 (Feb., 1954), 315.

17. "Nota sobre Lenormand," *Correo literario*, 20 (Mar. 15, 1951), 8.

18. "Estreno en ocho notas," *Correo literario*, III, 47 (May 1, 1952), 11.

19. "Puntos sobre las íes del Teatro Social," *Cuadernos hispanoamericanos*, 25 (Jan., 1952), 121.

20. "Tragedia," *Correo literario*, 70 (April 15, 1953), 10.

21. "Prefacio," in *Anatomía del realismo* (Barcelona, 1965), p. 7.

22. On the changing relevance of tragedy's social content see also Alfonso Sastre, "Tragedia 'antigua' y tragedia 'moderna,'" *Correo literario*, IV, 86 (Dec. 15, 1953), 10.

23. The notion of the "anonymous sin" is, of course, not original with Sastre. It is a conspicuous aspect of the thinking of many modern thinkers whose work Sastre has read: Kierkegaard, Heidegger, Unamuno, and Camus. The idea is explored in several of Sastre's own plays—especially *The Condemned Squad* and *The Blood of God.*

24. Sastre regards O'Neill as one of the twentieth century's major exponents of this tragic exaltation of human existence in its authentic mode (*Drama and Society,* pp. 141-44).

25. The première of *Death of a Salesman* in Madrid gave rise to an extended polemic between Sastre and Gonzalo Torrente Ballester, then drama critic for *Arriba,* a Madrid daily newspaper. Torrente's basic reaction to Miller's play had been: "The only thing I see in Loman is an imbecile." Sastre insisted that Loman was "a man who is painfully alive." The argument is summarized by both parties in "Polémica trasplantada," *Correo literario,* III, 43 (Mar. 1, 1952), 12. See also *Drama y sociedad,* pp. 97-99, 129-35; and Alfonso Sastre, "A propósito de 'La muerte de un viajante,' de Arthur Miller," *Cuadernos hispanoamericanos,* 27 (March, 1952), 454-56.

26. Sastre uses *Death of a Salesman* to illustrate this point (*Drama and Society,* p. 36).

27. Francis Fergusson, "Introduction," in Aristotle's *Poetics* (New York, 1961), p. 32.

28. *Ibid.,* p. 35.

29. Aristotle, *Poetics,* S. H. Butcher, trans. (New York, 1961), pp. 55-56.

30. *Ibid.,* pp. 52, 61, 75.

31. Francis Fergusson, "Introduction," p. 4.

32. S. H. Butcher, quoted in Francis Fergusson, "Introduction," p. 8.

33. Aristotle, *Poetics,* p. 68.

34. Francis Fergusson, "Introduction," p. 34.

35. Aristotle, *Poetics,* p. 68.

36. *Ibid.,* p. 69.

37. *Ibid.,* pp. 61-65.

38. Italics are Sastre's, as are those in all quotations unless otherwise indicated.

Chapter Three

1. Alfonso Sastre, "El teatro en la vida," *Informaciones* (March 18, 1959), p. 3.

2. *Ibid.*

3. Alfonso Sastre, "Siete notas sobre 'Esperando a Godot,'" *Primer acto,* 1 (April, 1957), 46-52.

4. *Ibid.,* p. 52.

5. *Ibid.*, p. 49.
6. *Ibid.*, p. 50.
7. Personal interview, December 29, 1964.
8. Alfonso Sastre, "Teatro épico, teatro dramático, teatro de vanguardia," *Indice,* XVII, 169 (Feb. 1, 1963), 8.
9. *Ibid.*
10. Alfonso Sastre, *Anatomía del realismo* (Barcelona, 1965), p. 40, n. 5.
11. Alfonso Sastre, "Notas del autor," in *La sangre y la ceniza,* p. ii. Unpublished manuscript, 1965, made available through courtesy of Alfonso Sastre.
12. Alfonso Sastre, "A modo de respuesta," *Primer acto,* 16 (Sept.-Oct., 1960), 2, n. 3.
13. Alfonso Sastre, "El teatro de Alfonso Sastre visto por Alfonso Sastre," *Primer acto,* 5 (Nov.-Dec., 1957), 7.
14. *Ibid.*
15. Alfonso Sastre, "Prefacio," in *Cuatro dramas de la revolución* (Madrid, 1963), p. 10.
16. *Ibid.*, p. 12.
17. Letter from Sastre to author, Dec. 29, 1964.
18. Luís Francisco Rebelo, "Introdução a uma leitura de Alfonso Sastre," in *Três peças de Alfonso Sastre* (Porto, 1961), p. 10.
19. Alfonso Sastre, "Tragedia y esperpento," *Primer acto,* 28 (Nov., 1961), 16.
20. For further comment on Sastre's liberalizing evolution, see Juan Emilio Aragonés, "El teatro profundizado de Alfonso Sastre," *Punta Europa,* VIII, 83 (March, 1963), 26.
21. José María de Quinto, "Un realismo de urgencia," in hand program for G.T.R. production of *En la red,* March, 1961.
22. Alfonso Sastre, "Teatro de la realidad," *Primer acto,* 18 (Dec., 1960), 2.
23. "Declaración del G.T.R."
24. "Teatro de la realidad," p. 2.
25. *Ibid.*
26. Alfonso Sastre, "Sobre lo exótico del drama," *Primer acto,* 7 (March-April, 1959), 51.
27. "Siete notas sobre 'Esperando a Godot,'" cited in note 3 of Chapter Three.
28. Sastre quoted in José R. Marra-López, "Alfonso Sastre, Narrador: Un nuevo realismo," *Insula,* 212-13 (July-Aug., 1964), 10.
29. See Martin Esslin, *The Theater of the Absurd* (Garden City, 1961), p. 34; and Jan Kott, "A Note on Beckett's Realism," *Tulane Drama Review,* X, 3 (Spring, 1966), 154-59.

30. Alfonso Sastre, *Anatomía del realismo* (Barcelona, 1965), p. 130. Other page references in this chapter to *Anatomy of Realism* will be included parenthetically in the text and will be designated by the abbreviation *AR*.

31. Georg Lukács, *Studies in European Realism* (New York, 1964), p. 6.

Chapter Four

1. Letter from Sastre to author, December 29, 1964.

2. Domingo Pérez Minik, "Alfonso Sastre: Ese dramaturgo español desplazado, provocador e inmolado," in Alfonso Sastre, *Obras completas* (Madrid, 1967), I, xxxix.

3. Years given in parentheses are the dates when plays were completed. *Pathetic Prologue*, however, was revised several times after the original completion date of 1950. See "Teatro de vanguardia, regreso al realismo y experiencia épica," in *Alfonso Sastre*, p. 142.

4. Examples: Nicolás González Ruiz, "Estreno de 'La mordaza,' en el Reina Victoria," *Ya* (Sept. 18, 1954), p. 7; Alfredo Marquerie, *Veinte años de teatro en España* (Madrid, 1959), pp. 201-2; Gonzalo Torrente Ballester, Review of *La mordaza*, in *Teatro español* (1954-1955), F. C. Sainz de Robles, ed. (Madrid, 1956), p. 32; Paul Werrie, "Où en est le théâtre espagnol?" *Écrits de Paris*, 182 (May, 1960), 114.

5. Alfonso Sastre, "Notas del autor," in *La sangre y la ceniza*, p. ii.

6. Letter from Sastre to author, December 29, 1964.

7. Alfonso Sastre, "El teatro de Alfonso Sastre visto por Alfonso Sastre," p. 7.

8. *Anatomía del realismo* (Barcelona, 1965), pp. 25-26.

9. "El teatro de Alfonso Sastre visto por Alfonso Sastre," p. 7. Although Sastre does not so specify, the equation of tragedy with the *investigación criminal* could actually be taken as another indication of the influence of Aristotle's *Poetics* on Sastre's thought. It will be recalled that Aristotle considered Sophocles' *Oedipus Rex* a model tragedy. This work is essentially a criminal investigation.

10. Letter from Sastre to author, December 29, 1964.

11. "Tiempo," in *Alfonso Sastre*, p. 67.

12. Leonard C. Pronko, "The 'Revolutionary Theatre' of Alfonso Sastre," *Tulane Drama Review*, V, 2 (Winter, 1960), 119.

13. See, for example, Francisco García Pavón, *Teatro social en España* (Madrid, 1962), p. 173; Angel Valbuena Prat, *Historia del teatro español* (Barcelona, 1956), p. 683; Paul Werrie, p. 117.

14. Pronko, pp. 119-20.

15. See Angel Del Río, *Historia de la literatura española,* rev. ed. (New York, 1963), II, 379-81; and García Pavón, pp. 173-79.

16. "Teatro de vanguardia, regreso al realismo y experiencia épica," p. 140.

17. See *Anatomía del realismo,* p. 26; " 'El cuervo' de Alfonso Sastre," *Indice*, XII, 108 (Jan., 1958), 17; Nicolás González Ruiz, "Estreno de 'El cuervo,' de Alfonso Sastre, en el María Guerrero," *Ya* (Nov. 1, 1957), p. 6; Pronko, p. 113.

18. "Autocrítica" to *En la red,* in *Teatro español* (1960-61), F. C. Sainz de Robles, ed. (Madrid, 1962), p. 249.

Chapter Five

1. *Death Has Sounded* and *Sleepwalker's Comedy* were written in collaboration with Medardo Fraile. However, Sastre was responsible for the plot of both these plays. Letter from Sastre to author, February 23, 1965.

2. De Coster, "Alfonso Sastre," *Tulane Drama Review,* V, 2 (Winter, 1960), 121-22.

3. Personal interview with Sastre, December 29, 1964. Also see Eugenio Garzo, "El teatro de Alfonso Sastre," *Cuadernos hispanoamericanos,* 59 (Nov., 1954), 214.

4. Alfonso Sastre and Medardo Fraile, *Ha sonado la muerte,* in *Teatro de vanguardia: 15 obras de Arte Nuevo* (Madrid, 1949), p. 177.

5. *Ibid.,* p. 198.

6. *Ibid.,* p. 187.

7. Alfonso Sastre, *Uranio 235,* in *Obras completas* (Madrid, 1967), I, 29. Subsequent quotations from plays not published in English translation will be made from this volume of Sastre's *Obras completas* (*Complete Works*), when the play in question is one that has been included in that collection. Page references to this volume will be included parenthetically in the text and will be designated by the symbol *OC*.

8. Personal interview with Quinto, March 24, 1965.

9. Domenech, "Tres obras de un autor revolucionario," in *Alfonso Sastre,* p. 40.

10. *Ibid.,* p. 39.

11. Maryvonne Rouxel, "Les Problèmes Sociaux dans l'oeuvre d'Alfonso Sastre" (thesis, Faculté des Lettres de Paris, Institut d'Études Hispaniques, 1964), p. 11.

12. Juan Emilio Aragonés, "El teatro profundizado de Alfonso Sastre," *Punta Europa,* VIII, 83 (March, 1963), 27.

13. Alfonso Sastre, "Prólogo," in *Ana Kleiber* (San Sebastián, 1957), p. 5.

14. Rouxel, p. 22.

15. Some critical reactions to *Anna Kleiber* may be found in "'Ana Kleiber' en Paris," *Primer acto*, 19 (Jan., 1961), 52; "'Ana Kleiber' d'Alfonso Sastre au théâtre Hébertot," *Le Canard Enchaîné*, 2114 (Apr. 26, 1961), 5; André Camp, "'Ana Kleiber' d'Alfonso Sastre," *L'Avant-Scène*, 243 (May 15, 1961), 36; Jean-Jacques Gautier, Review of *Ana Kleiber, Le Figaro* (Apr. 26, 1961), p. 22; Gabriel Marcel, "De New York à Barcelone," *Les Nouvelles Littéraires* (May 4, 1961), p. 10; Review of *Ana Kleiber, L'Express*, 516 (May 4, 1961), 49-50.

16. Alfonso Sastre, *Anna Kleiber*, Leonard C. Pronko, trans., in *The New Theatre of Europe*, Robert W. Corrigan, ed. (New York, 1962), p. 188. Subsequent quotations from *Anna Kleiber* are taken from this translation.

17. *Ana Kleiber, OC*, p. 475. My translation. The Pronko translation omits these lines.

18. Thierry Maulnier, "Le théâtre et son public," *Revue de Paris* (June, 1961), p. 133.

19. DeCoster, p. 131.

20. Sastre himself also dedicates a long and perplexing article to the problem of the relativity of time in the theater, and particularly in *The Raven*. See "Espacio-Tiempo y Drama," *Primer acto*, 6 (Jan.-Feb., 1958), 13-16.

21. In an allusion to this image of God in *The Raven* Sastre cites Nina's outburst at the end of Act Six in O'Neill's *Strange Interlude*: "I should be the happiest woman in the world! . . . only I better knock wood . . . before God the Father hears my happiness!" See "Deuda con Strindberg," *Primer acto*, 36 (Oct., 1962), 15.

22. "El teatro de Alfonso Sastre visto por Alfonso Sastre," p. 7.

23. René Burguera, "Ensayo sobre Sastre" (thesis, University of Grenoble, Faculté des Lettres et Sciences Humaines, n.d.), p. 21.

Chapter Six

1. *Anatomía del realismo*, p. 121.

2. The basic idea for *Community Bread* came from Sastre's reading of a poem by the Russian Pronia Kobilin, quoted by Juan Emilio Aragonés, "El teatro profundizado de Alfonso Sastre," p. 31. Sastre has confirmed Aragonés' assertion of this source: Personal interview, December 29, 1964.

3. "Nota del adaptor," in *Mulato* (Madrid, 1964), pp. 7-8.

4. Some ten years after he had written this play, from the vantage point of a more positive revolutionary philosophy, Sastre himself took note of *The Condemned Squad's* pessimistic implications: "Today . . . I think I would write *The Condemned Squad* somewhat differently. It would continue to be a condemnation of war, its rationales, and

its instigators. And perhaps the final scene—resigned and depressing—would take the form of an awakening, and Luis would not end up a poor lad who must prepare to live out his life as an absurd punishment" (*OC*, 162).

5. The metaphor "bridge" should not be understood here in a chronological sense. It will be recalled that three dramas of frustration were written after *The Condemned Squad.*

6. This fact is common knowledge in Madrid's theater circles. It has been confirmed by Sastre himself (personal interview, May 18, 1965); by Anthony M. Pasquariello, "Alfonso Sastre: Dramatist with a Mission," in *Escuadra hacia la muerte,* Anthony M. Pasquariello, ed. (New York, 1967), p. 5; and by Ricardo Domenech, "Tres obras de un autor revolucionario," in *Alfonso Sastre,* p. 37.

7. "Alfonso Sastre y las trágicas preguntas," *Alcalá,* 28-29 (Mar. 25, 1953), n.p.

8. *Ibid.*

9. "El teatro profundizado de Alfonso Sastre," p. 28.

10. "Hablando de 'Escuadra hacia la muerte,'" *Revista española,* 1 (May-June, 1953), 119.

11. Sastre quoted in Aragonés, "El teatro profundizado de Alfonso Sastre," p. 28.

12. This interpretation is also suggested by Leonard C. Pronko, *op. cit.,* p. 114; and by Anthony M. Pasquariello, "Censorship in the Spanish Theater and Alfonso Sastre's 'The Condemned Squad,'" *The Theater Annual,* XIX (1962), 25, n. 11.

13. Eduardo Haro Tecglen, Review of *Escuadra hacia la muerte, Informaciones* (Mar. 19, 1953), p. 7.

14. José María García Escudero, "Tiempo," p. 68.

15, Personal interview with Quinto, March 24, 1965.

16. Alfonso Sastre, "Posfácio pelo autor" (1960), in *Três peças de Alfonso Sastre,* Egito Gonçalves, trans. (Porto, 1961), p. 172.

17. "The 'Revolutionary Theatre' of Alfonso Sastre," p. 115.

18. Most of the play's critics recognized that the profession of José Alba was unimportant, but some reviewers and a significant number of spectators were unwilling or unable to recognize this fact. Thus, in a few instances a disproportionate emphasis was placed on inaccuracies in the behavior and statements of Marcos and Alba. *Aficionados* were apparently unwilling to forgive the liberties Sastre took with details of the bullfighting ritual. See V. Fernández Asís, Review of *La cornada, Pueblo* (Jan. 15, 1960), p. 20; Pablillos, "Corro de espectadores en el Teatro Lara," *Pueblo,* (Jan. 15, 1960), p. 20; Paul Werrie, "Où en est le théâtre espagnol?" *Écrits de Paris,* 182 (May, 1960), 118.

19. See Adolfo Prego, Review of *La cornada,* in *Teatro español* (1959-60), Federico Carlos Sainz de Robles, ed. (Madrid, 1961), p. 165.

20. *Ibid.,* p. 166.

21. Alfonso Sastre, *Death Thrust,* Leonard C. Pronko, trans., in *Masterpieces of the Modern Spanish Theatre,* Robert W. Corrigan, ed. (New York, 1967), pp. 252-53.

22. Alfonso Sastre, "Ante el estreno de 'La cornada,'" (1959), in *Tres dramas españoles* (Paris, 1965), p. 88.

23. In fact, Sastre originally intended to entitle this work *La cornada del hambre.* See Rafael Vázquez Zamora, "Autores de hoy y de mañana: Alfonso Sastre," *Insula,* XII, 130 (Sept., 1957), 10.

24. See Werrie, p. 118; and Gonzalo Torrente Ballester, Review of *La cornada,* in *Teatro español* (1959-60), p. 164. The controversial epilogue has been defended by Prego, p. 166; Olga Prjevalinsky Ferrer, "Three Years of Spanish Theater: 1960-63," *Books Abroad,* XXXVIII, 1 (Winter, 1964), 29; and José María Pemán, "El artículo de José María Pemán," *Primer acto,* 12 (Jan.-Feb., 1960), 13-15.

25. *Pathetic Prologue* was intended to be the first drama of a trilogy dealing with different phases of the revolutionary process. The remaining two works, however, were never written. Personal interview with Sastre, May 18, 1965.

26. "Teatro de vanguardia, regreso al realsimo y experiencia épica," p. 141.

27. There is a published English translation of *Pathetic Prologue* (see Bibliography). However, I have preferred not to draw upon it for my quotations. The translations of passages from *Pathetic Prologue* are my own.

28. "Teatro de vanguardia, regreso al realismo y experiencia épica," p. 140.

29. *Ibid.*

30. Sastre describes the emotional struggle he underwent in his attempt to resolve the drama's moral conflict. *Ibid.,* p. 142.

31. *Ibid.; OC,* pp. 102-3.

32. *OC,* p. 104.

33. Alfonso Sastre, "Autocrítica," in *Teatro español* (1960-61), Federico Carlos Sainz de Robles, ed. (Madrid, 1962), p. 249.

34. Adolfo Prego, Review of *En la red,* in *Teatro español* (1960-61), p. 250; and Rafael Vázquez Zamora, "'En la red,' de Alfonso Sastre," *Insula,* XVI, 173 (April, 1961), 15. Sastre is defended on this point by José Monleón, "Teatro en Madrid," *Primer acto,* 21 (March, 1961), 40.

35. Alfonso Sastre, "Autocrítica," p. 249.

36. *OC,* pp. 835-36. Leo's detailed enumeration of the atrocities committed against him was inspired by Henri Alleg, *La Question* (Paris, 1958). The pertinent passages from Alleg's work are reprinted, in Spanish, in *OC*, p. 796.

37. *OC,* pp. 825-26, 832-33, 835-36.

Chapter Seven

1. "Primeras notas para un encuentro con Bertolt Brecht," *Primer acto,* 13 (Mar.-Apr., 1960), 14.

2. I am not unaware that my use of the term "epic" to describe Sastre's new tendency may be questioned. The ambiguities of the term have been frequently noted by critics, and Brecht himself came to have serious doubts as to its clarity and appropriateness for the theater he advocated. Sastre has preferred to call his recent works "complex tragedies." His declared aim is not to write an "epic" theater at all, but to fuse and transcend both the theater of Brecht and the "dramatic" theater which he himself long cultivated in his dramas of penetrative realism. In spite of the term's deficiencies, however, I have elected to use it—for lack of a better alternative, and because I believe it is an essentially accurate way of describing Sastre's recent work and its relation to the twentieth-century theater.

3. Introductory note to *La taberna fantástica,* pp. iv-v. Unpublished manuscript, 1966, made available through the courtesy of Alfonso Sastre.

4. Introductory note to *Crónicas romanas,* n. p. Unpublished manuscript, 1968, made available through the courtesy of Alfonso Sastre.

5. There are numerous accounts of the life of Miguel Servet (Michael Servetus). Two of the more useful are Marcelino Menéndez y Pelayo, *Historia de los heterodoxos* (Madrid, 1956), I, 979-1040; and Will Durant, *The Story of Civilization* (New York, 1957), VI, 479-90. Sastre's own literary biography of Servet is discussed below, and Servet appears as a character in at least one other Spanish drama: *La muerte en los labios* (*Death on the Lips*), 1880, by José Echegaray.

6. Bertolt Brecht, *The Life of Galileo,* Desmond I. Vesey, trans. (London, 1963), p. 108.

7. *Ibid.*, p. 12.

8. *Ibid.*, p. 51.

9. *La sangre y la ceniza,* p. 151. Unpublished manuscript, 1965, made available through the courtesy of Alfonso Sastre.

Chapter Eight

1. Alfonso Sastre, *Flores rojas para Miguel Servet* (Madrid, 1967), p. 127.

2. It would perhaps be more accurate to say that *The 38th Parallel* is Sastre's "only separately published novel." Two of the three sections of *Lugubrious Nights* (below) might be regarded as short novels rather than as stories. Sastre's experimentation with generic hybrids complicates any attempt to categorize his prose works.

3. "Nota del adaptor," in *Mulato* (Madrid, 1964), p. 7.

4. "A las cinco de la tarde" is the screen version of *Death Thrust.*

5. "Algo así como un prólogo," in *El Paralelo 38* (Madrid, 1965), p. 8.

6. *Ibid.*, p. 7.

7. Alfonso Sastre, "Prefacio," in *Las noches lúgubres* (Madrid, 1964), p. 10.

8. I have left this last "quotation" in French, as it appears in the Spanish original, because the humorous effect of these lines depends largely on the fact that they are in a foreign language.

Selected Bibliography

(See Notes and References for further bibliographical orientation.)

PRIMARY SOURCES

1. Major Works of Alfonso Sastre

Alfonso Sastre. José Monleón, ed. Primer Acto Series (Madrid: Taurus, 1964). Includes *Cargo of Dreams, Pathetic Prologue,* and *Nocturnal Assault,* as well as a good collection of documents by and about Sastre.

Anatomía del realismo (Barcelona: Seix Barral, 1965).

Anna Kleiber. Leonard C. Pronko, trans., in *The New Theatre of Europe.* Robert W. Corrigan, ed. Delta Books (New York: Dell, 1962). English version of *Ana Kleiber.*

Cuatro dramas de la revolución (Madrid: Bullón, 1963). Includes *Community Bread, The Red Earth, Sad Are the Eyes of William Tell,* and *In the Net,* as well as a valuable introductory essay by Sastre.

Death Thrust. Leonard C. Pronko, trans., in *Masterpieces of the Modern Spanish Theatre.* Robert W. Corrigan, ed. (New York: Collier Books, 1967). English version of *La cornada.*

Drama y sociedad (Madrid: Taurus, 1956).

Flores rojas para Miguel Servet (Madrid: Rivadeneyra, 1967).

Guilherme Tell tem os olhos tristes (Lisbon: Prelo, 1965). Portuguese version of *Guillermo Tell tiene los ojos tristes.*

Las noches lúgubres (Madrid: Horizonte, 1964).

Obras completas (Madrid: Aguilar, 1967). Complete collection of Sastre's theater except for the epic plays. Also includes Sastre's commentaries on each play, plus a good introduction by Domingo Pérez Minik.

El Paralelo 38 (Madrid: La Novela Popular, 1965).

Pathetic Prologue. Leonard C. Pronko, trans., in *Modern International Drama,* I, 2 (March, 1968), 195-215. English version of *Prólogo patético.*

Il sangue e la cenere and *Nella rete.* María Luisa Aguirre and Dario Puccini, trans. (Milano: Feltrinelli, 1967). Italian versions of *La sangre y la ceniza* and *En la red,* plus good general introduction to Sastre and his work.

Teatro (Buenos Aires: Losada, 1960). Includes *The Condemned Squad, The Red Earth, Anna Kleiber, Death in the Neighborhood, Sad Are the Eyes of William Tell,* and *The Raven.*

Teatro de vanguardia: 15 obras de Arte Nuevo (Madrid: Permán, 1949). Includes *Death Has Sounded, Sleepwalker's Comedy, Cargo of Dreams,* and *Uranium 235.*

Teatro español. F. C. Sainz de Robles, ed. (Madrid: Aguilar, 1956, 1961, 1962, 1968). (Volumes for 1954-55, 1959-60, 1960-61, 1966-67.) Includes texts of *The Gag, Death Thrust, In the Net,* and *Office of Darkness,* plus reviews and commentaries on these plays.

Teatro selecto (Madrid: Escelicer, 1966). Includes *The Condemned Squad, The Gag, Anna Kleiber, The Blood of God, Sad Are the Eyes of William Tell, In the Net, Death Thrust.*

Tres dramas españoles. Colección Ebro (Paris: Librairie du Globe, 1965). Includes *The Garbage Pail, Death Thrust, Office of Darkness.*

Três peças de Alfonso Sastre. Egito Gonçalves, trans. (Porto: Divulgação, 1961). Portuguese versions of *Escuadra hacia la muerte, La mordaza,* and *El cuervo,* plus good introductory essay.

SECONDARY SOURCES

ALVARO, FRANCISCO. *El espectador y la crítica: El teatro en España en 1967* (Valladolid: Private printing, 1968). Some good pages on *Office of Darkness,* as well as consideration of all plays premièred in Madrid in the 1967 season.

ANDERSON, FARRIS F. *The Dialectics of Alfonso Sastre.* Diss., University of Wisconsin, 1968. Detailed study of *Anatomy of Realism* and of the influence of Sartre and Brecht on Sastre; extensive bibliography.

———. "Sastre on Brecht: The Dialectics of Revolutionary Theatre," *Comparative Drama,* III, 4 (Winter, 1969-70), 282-96. The evolution of Sastre's attitudes toward Brecht.

BUERO VALLEJO, ANTONIO. "Obligada precisión acerca del 'Imposibilismo,'" *Primer acto,* 15 (July-Aug., 1960), 1-6. Buero's side of the 1960 "Posibilismo" polemic with Sastre.

CASTAGNINO, RAÚL H. "Escuela de la realidad," *La Prensa* (May 29, 1966, n.p.). A good review and critique of *Anatomy of Realism.*

GORDÓN, JOSÉ. *Teatro experimental español* (Madrid: Escelicer, 1965). Interesting recollections of the Arte Nuevo adventure by one of the group's charter members.

MONLEÓN, JOSÉ, ed. *Alfonso Sastre.* Primer Acto Series (Madrid: Taurus, 1964). Good collection of documents by and about Sastre, as well as the texts of three of Sastre's plays.

PÉREZ MINIK, DOMINGO. *Teatro europeo contemporáneo* (Madrid: Guadarrama, 1961). Places Sastre's work in a European context.

SALVAT, RICARD. *El teatre contemporani* (Barcelona: Edicions 62, 1966), II, 231-36. Compact appraisal of Sastre's work by a perceptive Catalonian critic.

VÁZQUEZ ZAMORA, RAFAEL. "Alfonso Sastre no acepta el 'Posibilismo,'" *Insula,* XV, 164-65 (July-Aug., 1960), 27. Sastre's principle of "Imposibilismo" that led to the bitter exchange with Buero in 1960.

VILLEGAS M., JUAN. "La acción dramática y la Estructura Temporal en 'Ana Kleiber' de Alfonso Sastre," in *Hacia un método de análisis de la obra dramática,* pp. 201-54 (Valdivia: Imprenta de la Universidad Austral de Chile, 1963). Thorough analysis of Sastre's manipulation of time in *Anna Kleiber.*

———. "La sustancia metafísica de la tragedia y su función social: *Escuadra hacia la muerte* de Alfonso Sastre," *Symposium,* XXI, 3 (Fall, 1967), 255-62. Fairly helpful introductory study of *The Condemned Squad.*

Index

Aldecoa, Ignacio, 17
Anatomy of Realism (*Anatomía del realismo*), 16, 42, 50, 55-63, 65, 129-30, 137
Anna Kleiber (*Ana Kleiber*), 70, 77-79, 137
Antoine, André, 31, 32, 37, 51, 52, 53, 54
Aristotle, 28, 30, 33-34, 39-42, 58, 64, 67 fn. 9, 71, 116, 117, 130, 131
Arte Nuevo, 14, 15, 16, 73-76, 77

Banquet, The (*El banquete*), 70, 71, 119-21, 132, 137
Beckett, Samuel, 44-47, 51, 53-54, 57, 69, 75
Betti, Ugo, 13, 25, 26
The Blood and the Ashes (*La sangre y la ceniza*), 65, 70, 71, 123, 124-29, 130, 132, 133, 134, 144
The Blood of God (*La sangre de Dios*), 70, 77, 81-83, 144
Bousoño, Carlos, 17
Brecht, Bertolt, 15, 18, 37, 46, 57, 58, 60, 65, 71, 116-19, 123, 125, 126-27, 130, 137

Cargo of Dreams (*Cargamento de sueños*), 65, 70, 75-76, 77
Castro, Fidel, 16
Censorship, 13, 15, 16, 91, 97-98, 120
Cervantes, Miguel de, 123, 134-36
Community Bread (*El pan de todos*), 64, 65, 70, 71, 86-87, 109
The Condemned Squad (*Escuadra hacia la muerte*), 16, 64, 70, 89-96, 97, 98, 99, 109, 131, 144
Costas, Carlos José, 14

Death Has Sounded (*Ha sonado la muerte*), 70, 73, 74
Death in the Neighborhood (*Muerte en el barrio*), 70, 71, 89, 100-102, 131
Death Thrust (*La cornada*), 70, 71, 89, 100, 102-6, 119, 120
Drama and Society (*Drama y sociedad*), 16, 20, 23-42, 43, 44, 49, 50, 51, 52, 53, 57, 58, 59, 60, 65, 94, 137

Fantastic Tavern, The (*La taberna fantástica*), 70, 71, 119, 121-22, 130, 132, 138
Four Dramas of Revolution (*Cuatro dramas de la revolución*), 65, 109
Fraile, Medardo, 14, 73 fn. 1
Franco, José, 14

G. T. R. (Grupo de Teatro Realista), 16, 51-53, 57
Gag, The (*La mordaza*), 16, 65, 70, 71, 89, 96-100, 109, 131
Galileo, 126-27
Garbage Pail, The (*El cubo de la basura*), 70, 71, 85-86
García Lorca, Federico, 13
Generation of 1898, 13
Gordón, José, 14
Goytisolo, Juan, 17
Guía, 15

Heidegger, Martin, 35, 36 fn. 23, 43
Hierro, José, 17
La Hora, 15

In the Net (*En la red*), 16, 64, 65, 70, 71, 107, 109, 111-15, 131

Jardiel Poncela, Enrique, 24, 25

Kierkegaard, Soren, 36 fn. 23, 81

Lenormand, Henri, 25, 26
Lope de Vega, 110
Lugubrious Nights (*Las noches lúgubres*), 54, 65, 139-43, 144
Lukács, Georg, 18, 60, 62

Maeterlinck, Maurice, 25, 26
Matute, Ana María, 17
Miller, Arthur, 15, 28, 34, 37, 42, 67
Monleón, José, 17
Muñiz, Carlos, 16, 17

Naturalism, 32, 52, 54, 63, 129-30, 131
Nocturnal Assault (*Asalto nocturno*), 65, 70, 71, 119, 120, 130

Office of Darkness (*Oficio de tinieblas*), 70, 71, 86, 130
Olmo, Lauro, 17
O'Neill, Eugene, 15, 25, 26, 28, 34, 35, 42, 65, 81 fn. 21
Otero, Blas de, 17

Palacios, José María, 14
Paso, Alfonso, 14, 17
Pathetic Prologue (*Prólogo patético*), 64, 65, 70, 71, 107-9, 131
"Penetrative" realism (*realismo profundizado*), 29, 31, 32, 33, 37, 42, 50, 54, 60-63, 67, 71, 84-85, 115, 117 fn. 2, 131
Pirandello, Luigi, 16
Primer acto, 15, 44

Quinquilleros, 121-22, 138
Quinto, José María de, 14, 15, 16, 17, 20, 21, 51, 75, 97

The Raven (*El cuervo*), 65, 69, 70, 77, 79-81, 140, 144
Red Earth, The (*Tierra roja*), 65, 70, 71, 107, 109-111, 131
Red Flowers for Miguel Servet (*Flores rojas para Miguel Servet*), 133-36, 144
Rice, Elmer, 15, 37
Roman Chronicles (*Crónicas romanas*), 65, 70, 71, 123-24, 130, 132

Sad Are the Eyes of William Tell (*Guillermo Tell tiene los ojos tristes*), 65, 70, 71, 86, 87-89, 125, 130, 131, 144
Sánchez Ferlosio, Rafael, 17
Sartre, Jean-Paul, 15, 18, 21, 22, 28, 35, 37, 42, 43, 65, 67, 69, 93, 94, 108
Screenplays (Sastre's), 137
Servet, Miguel (Michael Servetus), 119, 125-29, 133-36, 144
Sinclair, Upton, 28, 37, 67
Sleepwalker's Comedy (*Comedia sonámbula*), 70, 73
Spanish Civil War, 13, 14, 17
Spanish theater, criticism of, 14, 15, 16, 18-19, 20, 21, 23, 24, 53, 57, 123

T. A. S. (Teatro de Agitación Social), 15, 16
Theater of the Absurd, 46
The 38th Parallel (*El paralelo 38*), 136-39
Tragedy, 22-23, 25, 26, 29, 33, 34-42, 47, 48, 49-51, 53, 57, 59, 61-62, 67, 109, 117 fn. 2, 123

Unamuno, Miguel de, 13, 28, 35, 36 fn. 23
Uranium 235 (*Uranio 235*), 65, 70, 73, 74-75, 108

Weiss, Peter, 18, 123-24, 125
Wells, H. G., 74
Wilder, Thornton, 37, 73, 74